The Gospel According to Joseph Smith

The Gospel According to Joseph Smith

A Christian Response to Mormon Teaching

Ethan E. Harris

Foreword by
Bill McKeever

P.O. BOX 817 • PHILLIPSBURG • NEW JERSEY 08865-0817

Scripture quotations are from the King James Version, from *The Official Scriptures of the Church of Jesus Christ of Latter-day Saints* (Salt Lake City: Intellectual Reserve, Inc., 2000).

Page design byTobias Design

Typesetting by Lakeside Design Plus

Printed in the United States of America

Library of Congress Cataloging-in-Publication Data

Harris, Ethan E., 1969-
The Gospel according to Joseph Smith : a Christian response to Mormon teaching / Ethan E. Harris ; foreword by Bill McKeever.
p. cm.
Includes biliographical references (p.) and index.
ISBN 0-87552-180-0
1. Smith, Joseph, 1805-1844. 2. Church of Jesus Christ of Latter-Day Saints—Apologetic works. 3. Church of Jesus Christ of Latter-Day Saints—Doctrines. 4. Mormon Church—Apologetic works. 5. Mormon Church—Doctrines. 6. Church of Jesus Christ of Latter-day Saints. I. Title.

BX8635.5 .H37 2001
230'.93—dc21

2001021396

This book is dedicated to

DRS. GARY DERICKSON AND RICHARD CAULKINS

who have tried to teach me how to
humbly read the Bible and
think clearly.

CONTENTS

FOREWORD

The Gospel. The Good News. Those who have experienced its effect see it as an act of infinite grace and mercy on an undeserving world. To think that the God of all creation would consider the plight of sinful mankind, step into time, and volunteer to pay man's sin-debt has kept Christian believers in awe for centuries. To be sure, Christ came into the world to save sinners. He bestowed His mercy and displayed His unlimited patience, and as a result, millions who have offended His righteousness have come to believe and receive His gift of eternal life. For this we can't help but give God honor and glory for ever and ever.

History demonstrates that man has a way of corrupting what is good and pure. It didn't take long before even the Gospel itself was considered in need of "revision." Down through the ages a multitude of people, some well-meaning, others outright evil, have attempted to tamper with the Good News of God's salvation. Unfortunately, that which is not the pure and perfect Gospel is, as stated by the Apostle Paul, "no gospel at all."

Probably no other American religion has been as colorful and controversial as the Church of Jesus Christ of Latter-day Saints. From its humble beginnings in the backwoods of New York, this organization has become a major player in the realm of world religions. Though many see Mormonism as just another Christian denomination, the LDS Church makes no such claim for itself. From the beginning its founder, Joseph Smith, insisted that his church was "the only true and living church upon the face of the whole earth," the only church with which God is "well pleased." To the majority of Mormons, those who profess to be Christians but are not members of the LDS Church are, in actuality, a part of what they call the Great Apostasy.

Discerning the differences between Mormonism and Christianity has not always been easy. Because Mormons use a vocabulary that is very similar to that used by professing Christians, it has been difficult for some to see the vast difference in the doctrinal positions held by the two groups. Because Mormons often speak of the "Heavenly Father," the "Savior," "salvation by grace," "the Scriptures," and being "born again," many have assumed that the disparities are only minimal and should not cause any alarm. The fact of the matter is that Smith and his successors have devised a religious system that falls far short of Christian orthodoxy.

The Body of Christ can no longer ignore the presence of the LDS Church. To do so in light of its rapid growth would be irresponsible. It behooves all Christians to better understand what motivates our LDS friends and relatives if we are going to effectively dialogue with them.

The volume you hold in your hand will help you quickly sift through the language barrier and enhance your understanding of this complex religion. By citing primary sources,

Ethan Harris allows the leaders of the LDS Church to explain the positions of their church in their own words. It should grieve us as Christians to see how far these men have strayed from the Truth. To know that millions of people have embraced their error should also cause us great concern. It should also give us a resolve to defend what we believe to be true to all who may ask. It is our prayer that this book, like any tool, will be used wisely and for the glory of God.

Bill McKeever
Mormonism Research Ministry

PREFACE

The many inconsistencies that lie within the teachings of the Church of Jesus Christ of Latter-day Saints (LDS) will be exposed in the following pages. This is in no way an exhaustive compilation of difficulties facing the Mormon Church, but is an effort to underscore some of the most problematic areas.

The method of this study is to give a general overview of foundational teachings from the texts of Mormonism and its Prophets. We will, by way of contrast, cite authorities within that community and biblical passages that are in contradiction with them. We will explicate "The LDS View" and then see how "The Biblical View" opposes it.

We will also see that though many members of the Mormon Church claim absolute allegiance to their Church, a vast majority of them are not fully aware of the official Church teaching on a wide variety of doctrines. Additionally, we will point out the hostility of Mormon leaders toward Christianity and the manufacturing of misinformation to val-

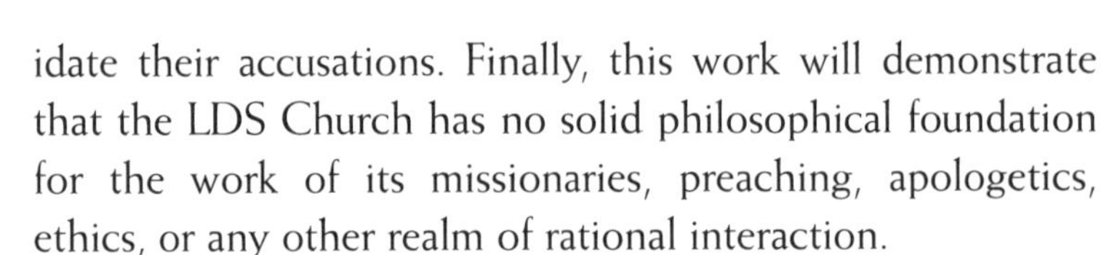

idate their accusations. Finally, this work will demonstrate that the LDS Church has no solid philosophical foundation for the work of its missionaries, preaching, apologetics, ethics, or any other realm of rational interaction.

Official Mormon doctrine is something of an elusive entity. Most doctrine passed along to non-Mormons is confined to what is common knowledge among LDS members. The doctrines of Mormon Prophets that are not considered popular are usually not mentioned or discussed in public.

Other than the book *Mormon Doctrine,* written by the Mormon Apostle Bruce R. McConkie, there does not appear to be any formal systemization of the doctrine of the LDS Church. Many scholars from Brigham Young University and freelance writers have attempted to represent official LDS teaching over the years. The problem is that their writings are not accepted by the LDS community as binding or as divinely inspired. They do not officially represent the teachings of the Mormon Prophets or the Standard Works.

The Mormon Church not only has been diverted from the biblical understanding of truth, but also has deviated from many teachings of the *Book of Mormon,* which is the foundation of the Latter-day Saints belief system. This may be seen in the many contradictory statements made by later teachers and in documents written after the *Book of Mormon* was made available. Our quotation of various passages will demonstrate contradictions within the teachings of the sacred texts and authorities of the Mormon Church. To counter the charge of taking quotes out of context, I challenge the reader to read all Scripture and other quotations in the original sources.

God has given us an opportunity to be involved in the lives of those around us. We should find satisfaction in bringing His Word to others just as others have been used to bring His Word to us. Study of His Word should bring us understanding through the Holy Spirit's guidance, and we should subject all of our thoughts and beliefs to rigorous scriptural analysis. Accordingly, the use of LDS materials in this volume is not meant to defame the LDS Church, its members, and its leaders, but to emphasize the points of departure from the Scriptures of the Old and New Testaments.

By studying and examining the doctrines and various teachings of the Mormon Church, we Christians can indicate to Mormons that we are open to taking up the challenge and evaluating their message. That their message sounds spiritual or mystical does not in itself make that message spiritual or true. Maybe their teaching is false, maybe it isn't; but how will we know without prayer and study?

It is our hope to come to a greater understanding of the differences between the Latter-day Saints and those who disagree with their beliefs, and to aid anyone who is studying the teachings of the Mormon Church to test their validity in the light of the Old and New Testaments. With prayerful study and patience, may we come to a knowledge of the Truth that God has delivered to the universal Church through Jesus Christ the Messiah.

The God of the Bible is much more than the man-centered religion of the Mormon Church claims. He is holy and perfect, and we are His creation. I was once asked by a very gracious LDS man, "What is the point of your faith if you cannot become a god?" I told him that the end goal was to worship God and enjoy Him forever. He laughed.

It is my sincere conviction that most of the Mormons with whom I have spoken do not show a deep desire to worship and praise Christ. They believe they love the Lord.

They claim that they praise God. But the words of the gentleman I cited are typical of what many Mormons really feel about worshipping God. I usually come away depressed after a personal conversation with LDS members. I want them to know the joy of knowing the Christ of the Scriptures. It hurts me when they fail to understand and accept His true nature.

The first two chapters give preliminary information that is necessary as a foundation. We will present statements by Mormon officials and passages from Scripture that encourage serious study of all materials that we are given. We will also see the bias that many LDS members hold against Christians. Christians are often seen as liars who distort the doctrines of the Mormon Church.

The next section, chapters 3–7, presents a brief discussion of Mormonism, an external critique of LDS doctrine as viewed from the standpoint of biblical Christianity. We will note many differences of doctrine between Christian and Mormon theology. Chapter 8, an internal critique of LDS philosophy, focuses on the weaknesses of Mormonism from an ethical perspective. In chapter 9 we conclude by reprinting a number of testimonies of Christians who have left the Mormon Church and the difficulties that they faced in their decisions to leave.

Our conviction is that the Church of Jesus Christ of Latter-day Saints cannot logically respond to our critique, nor can it comport with the ethical claims that it has made. Since it is not based on an absolute concept of God, the LDS Church has no ultimate foundation for much of its work and theology.

ACKNOWLEDGMENTS

It is amazing to discover how many people it takes to complete a book. Without the many hours of effort by others, this work would never have been possible. I would like to express my gratitude to them in this short space.

Let me first extend appreciation to my wife, Mindi, and her mother, Mary Lynn Twombly, for burying themselves in the manuscript, hunting out grammatical errors, in an attempt to make me sound coherent. Keith Mathison read through the manuscript multiple times and made numerous suggestions that enhanced the flow of the work. Without the encouragement of R. C. and Vesta Sproul, Al Fisher, and Alan Yardis, this title would never have gone to print.

More than all, I would like to thank Lane Thuet and Bill McKeever. Lane spent untold hours clarifying, proofing, checking references, making suggestions, and offering criticisms that have made this title more successful that I could have made it myself.

Many others have played an important part whom I would also thank: the editorial staff of P&R for making needed corrections; Nevin Mawhinney, Burk Parsons, Jim Spradlin, and Terry Groner; those who have graced this book with their endorsements; LDS members I have met along the way; and others I haven't the space to acknowledge by name. Thank you.

PROPHETS (PRESIDENTS) OF THE LDS CHURCH

		BORN	BECAME PROPHET	DIED
1	Joseph Smith	1805	1830	1844
2	Brigham Young	1801	1847	1877
3	John Taylor	1808	1880	1887
4	Wilford Woodruff	1807	1889	1898
5	Lorenzo Snow	1814	1898	1901
6	Joseph F. Smith	1838	1901	1918
7	Heber J. Grant	1856	1918	1945
8	George Albert Smith	1870	1945	1951
9	David O. McKay	1873	1951	1970
10	Joseph Fielding Smith	1876	1970	1972
11	Harold B. Lee	1899	1972	1973
12	Spencer W. Kimball	1895	1973	1985
13	Ezra Taft Benson	1899	1985	1994
14	Howard W. Hunter	1907	1994	1995
15	Gordon B. Hinckley	1910	1995	

1

SETTING THE STAGE

We begin our examination of Mormonism by encouraging both LDS and non-LDS to seriously study what we are taught by others and to compare those teachings to Scripture. For a person, group, or organization to claim authority from God does not necessarily prove that their teachings are true. If Scripture is our ultimate authority, all human words should be subject to verification by God's Word. There must be a standard from which we may determine truth. Studying to show ourselves approved of God should be the goal of all who profess the name of Christ (2 Tim. 2:15).

The Mormon Prophet Brigham Young challenged all people to compare the teaching of the Mormon Church to the Bible:

> I say to the whole world, receive the truth, no matter who presents it to you. Take up the Bible, com-

> pare the religion of the Latter-day Saints with it, and see if it will stand the test.[1]

The Mormon Prophet Joseph Fielding Smith lamented that so many members of the Mormon Church would not study the Standard Works:

> It is a regret to be under the necessity of saying that too many of the members of the Church are mentally lazy so far as seeking the words of life. We have been commanded to search the commandments in the Doctrine and Covenants; we have been commanded to study the Book of Mormon, and the Lord has blessed us with the Pearl of Great Price, all in addition to what the world for nearly two thousand years and more has had.[2]

A recent Mormon Prophet, Ezra Taft Benson, echoed the words of his predecessors:

> We urge you to study the Book of Mormon as individuals and families and then to do as the Prophet Nephi counseled: liken the Scriptures to yourselves so that it will be for your profit and learning (see 1 Nephi 19:23–24).[3]

The biblical book of Acts gives an account of the Bereans' response to the teachings of Paul:

> And the brethren immediately sent away Paul and Silas by night unto Berea: who coming thither went into the synagogue of the Jews. These were more

> noble than those in Thessalonica, in that they received the word with all readiness of mind, and searched the scriptures daily, whether those things were so. Therefore many of them believed; also of honourable women which were Greeks, and of men, not a few. (Acts 17:10–12)

In the closing remarks of his first letter to the Thessalonians, Paul encourages the Church to test his words by Scripture:

> Prove all things; hold fast that which is good. Abstain from all appearance of evil. (1 Thess. 5:21–22)

In another letter, 2 Timothy, Paul tells us how we should respond to those who oppose us:

> And the servant of the Lord must not strive; but be gentle unto all men, apt to teach, patient. In meekness instructing those that oppose themselves; if God peradventure will give them repentance to the acknowledging of the truth; And that they may recover themselves out of the snare of the devil, who are taken captive by him at his will. (2 Tim. 2:24–26)

The Apostle Peter tells us what those who love the Lord must be like. Notice the manner in which we are supposed to approach others:

> But sanctify the Lord God in your hearts: and be ready always to give an answer to every man that asketh you a reason of the hope that is in you with

> meekness and fear: Having a good conscience; that, whereas they speak evil of you, as of evil doers, they may be ashamed that falsely accuse your good conversation in Christ. (1 Peter 3:15–16)

One final admonition from the Apostle John stresses the need to distinguish with certainty between what God has delivered as Truth and those words that false prophets have proposed:

> Beloved, believe not every spirit, but try the spirits whether they are of God: because many false prophets are gone out unto the world. (1 John 4:1)

We must always carefully examine the doctrine and various teachings that are presented to us. All Scripture must be studied in context to get a full understanding of what the writer means. Even the passages quoted above should be checked in the Bible for their context. Challenge yourself to look up and verify the context of all citations of Scripture that are used in your Church or in discussions with others. If the context does not support an interpretation that is being presented, we must be cautious about the doctrine in question.

Hate or Compassion?

Before we enter our brief study of Mormonism, we must be aware of the potential hostility that awaits Christians who wish to share the Gospel with Mormons. Mormons are generally very concerned about the impression that the outside world has of them. Mormon missionaries make it clear that their Church does not criticize other beliefs. They also take pains to show how compassionate they are in the face of opposition. But we must remember what the consensus of Mormons really is regarding Christians: Christians are apostate.

The claim is still frequently made that the LDS community has never engaged in name-calling or insulting other religions. Mormon Prophets have stressed the need for humility and decency in dialogue with people who disagree with their belief system. We must likewise stress that simple argumentation should not be seen as slanderous. Asking for discussion and debate does not necessitate hostility and antagonistic dispute. Issues can be discussed without hatred for the opposite viewpoint.

Heber J. Grant, one of the early LDS Prophets, emphasized the need for Mormons not to criticize anyone but themselves:

> I have given much advice to the Latter-day Saints in my time, and one of the principal items was never to criticize anyone but ourselves. I believe in fault-finding for breakfast, dinner and supper, but only with our own dear selves.[4]

Brigham Young, the second LDS Prophet, thought it was wise not to judge anyone, but to let God do the judging because only He has full knowledge of the world:

> I am very thankful that it is not our province, in our present condition, to judge the world; if it were, we would ruin everything. We have not sufficient wis-

> dom; our minds are not filled with the knowledge and power of God; the spirit needs to contend with the flesh a little more until it shall be successful in subduing its passions, until the whole soul is brought into perfect harmony with the mind and will of God. And we must also acquire the discretion that God exercises in being able to look into futurity, and to ascertain and know the results of our acts away in the future, even in eternity, before we will be capable of judging.[5]

Spencer W. Kimball, another LDS Prophet, made a pointed statement about how people respond to each other:

> Therefore, we often judge wrongfully if we try to fathom their meaning and give our own interpretation to it.[6]

Ezra Taft Benson, one of the more recent Prophets of the LDS Church, believed that in order to evangelize non-Mormons, one should be patient and not critical:

> Let us exhort each other to fulfill our missionary responsibility. Let us do it with love—not criticism. Let us do it with understanding—not berating. But let us do it, and do it with urgency. Let us catch the vision and the inspiration of President Spencer W. Kimball. We need to understand that member-missionary work is literally the key to the future growth of the Church and that we have covenanted with our Father in Heaven to do this work.[7]

While most of us would agree with many of these comments by the Mormon Prophets, it is astounding to find that many of the LDS Prophets have openly criticized Christians with a great deal of hostility and malice. Although LDS Prophets have called for compassion to non-Mormons, they often do not apply this teaching to themselves. Consider a few of the claims that Mormon leaders have made regarding those who in the past two millennia have called on the name of Christ.

Brigham Young, the second Prophet of the LDS Church, gives us his view of Christians:

> The Christian world, I discovered, was like the captain and crew of a vessel on the ocean without a compass, and tossed to and fro whithersoever the wind listed to blow them. When the light came to me, I saw that all the so-called Christian world was groveling in darkness.[8]

There are various other fine examples of Young's open slander against the non-Mormon world:

> While Brother Taylor was speaking of the sectarian world, it occurred to my mind that the wicked do not know any more than the dumb brutes, comparatively speaking; but it is our business to hunt up and gather out all the honest portion of the nations of the earth, and give them salvation. We may very properly say that the sectarian world do not know anything correctly, so far as pertains to salvation. Ask them where heaven is? where they are going to when they die? where Paradise is? and there is not a

> priest in the world that can answer your questions. Ask them what kind of a being our Heavenly Father is, and they cannot tell you so much as Balaam's ass told him. They are more ignorant than children.[9]

> The arts and sciences are somewhat advanced among the Christian nations; but as to a true knowledge of things as they are in eternity, there never were nations more ignorant. According to my definition of the word, a people are heathenish that do not know things as they ought. The Christian world, so called, are heathens as to their knowledge of the salvation of God.[10]

> With regard to true theology, a more ignorant people never lived than the present so-called Christian world.[11]

Clearly, Young shows a high level of negativity toward Christians. In yet another instance he supports the charge that Christians are hatched in Hell:

> Brother Taylor has just said that the religions of the day were hatched in Hell. The eggs were laid in Hell, hatched on its borders, and then kicked on to the earth. They may be called cockatrices, for they sting wherever they go. Go to their meetings in the Christian world, and mingle in their society, and you will hear them remark, Our ministers dictate our soul's salvation; and they are perfectly composed and resigned to trust their whole future destiny to their priests, though they durst not trust them with

> one single dollar beyond their salaries and a few presents. They can trust their eternal welfare in the hands of their priests, but hardly dare trust them with so much as a bushel of potatoes. Is that principle here? Yes, more or less.[12]

In this refutation of Christianity, Young suggests that the major fault of Christians is their willingness to accept the words of their ministers.[13] However, one would be hard-pressed to identify a Christian Church whose members believe that their pastor controls and dictates their eternal salvation. It would be more proper to lay this charge against the Mormon Church or any other group that claims that biblical Truth comes from its organization alone.

Our final examples come from the words of the third Prophet, John Taylor:

> There is no nation now that acknowledges that hand of God; there is not a king, potentate, nor ruler that acknowledges his jurisdiction. We talk about Christianity, but it is a perfect pack of nonsense. Men talk about civilization; but I do not want to say much about that, for I have seen enough of it. Myself and hundreds of the Elders around me have seen its pomp, parade, and glory; and what is it? It is a sounding brass and a tinkling cymbal; it is as corrupt as Hell; and the Devil could not invent a better engine to spread his work than the Christianity of the nineteenth century.[14]

> The transactions of men are even more outrageous against the Lord, and the only excuse for them is

> their ignorance. What! are Christians ignorant? Yes, as ignorant of the things of God as the brute beast.[15]

> And Christianity, at the present time, is no more enlightened than other systems have been. What does the Christian world know about God? Nothing; yet these very men assume the right and power to tell others what they shall and what they shall not believe in. Why, so far as the things of God are concerned, they are the veriest fools; they know neither God nor the things of God.[16]

Clearly, Mormon Prophets have not shown much compassion in their teachings about Christianity. These are public statements made with extremely hostile feelings. Earlier, we read statements by Mormon Prophets urging Mormons not to criticize or think less of those who do not agree with LDS teaching. Yet, at the same time, these Prophets denied their own words and spoke with great hostility and insensitivity toward Christians. May we, as Christians, not respond to unbelievers as in the examples above.

If we truly believe that people are lost, how should we respond to them? Unbelief is surely not a laughing matter. We must not be arrogant in our belief. If we are to boast, let us boast in the grace of the Lord Jesus Christ, who saves us from sin and condemnation.

A Short History

Bruce McConkie in his work *Mormon Doctrine* identifies the origin of the nickname "Mormon." It came from the ancient Nephite prophet, Mormon, who compiled and abridged the sacred records of his people under the title *Book of Mormon.*[17] The nickname is given to those who believe the *Book of Mormon* to be a true account of Jesus Christ and the inhabitants of ancient America. The title "Mormon" is not offensive to most members of the Latter-day Saints Church.

The origin of the Church of Jesus Christ of Latter-day Saints is a somewhat recent occurrence. Joseph Smith, the founder and first Prophet of the LDS Church, was born on December 23, 1805, in Sharon, Vermont. According to the account that appears in the *History of the Church,* Smith in 1838 reflected on how the events in his earlier life came to be used by God. In 1820, having encountered Methodists, Presbyterians, and Baptists fighting against each other in a war of words and tumult of opinions, he yearned to find out which of the prevalent religious beliefs of his day were correct.[18] After reading James 1:5 ("If any of you lack wisdom, let him ask of God"), Joseph went into the woods near his home and prayed to God to reveal which of these groups was correct or if any was correct at all. Being just fourteen years old, Joseph now for the first time prayed to God out loud. No sooner had he done so than a pillar of light appeared and came down on him. He later claimed that two beings descended and stood above him in the air.

> One of them spake unto me, calling me by name, and said—pointing to the other—THIS IS MY BELOVED SON, HEAR HIM.[19]

Joseph asked these two personages which of the sects was correct; he was told that none of them was correct and to join none of them.

Joseph Smith's second vision took place on September 21, 1823. While he was lying in his bed in prayer, a bright light filled the room and a messenger appeared. The messenger revealed his name as Moroni. The Angel's mission was to instruct Joseph to retrieve Golden Plates that contained the history of the

> former inhabitants of this continent, and the sources from whence they sprang. He also said that the fullness of the everlasting Gospel was contained in it, as delivered by the Savior to the ancient inhabitants; also that there were two stones in silver bows—and these stones, fastened to a breastplate, constituted what is called the Urim and Thummim—deposited with the plates; and the possession and use of these stones were what constituted "seers" in ancient or former times; and that God had prepared them for the purpose of translating the book.[20]

Joseph was directed to go to the site where Moroni had buried the Golden Plates:

> [It] is located between Palmyra and Manchester in the western part of the state of New York . . . (Morm. 6; Ether 15). Joseph Smith, Oliver Cowdery, and many of the early brethren, who were familiar with all the circumstances attending the coming forth of the *Book of Mormon* in this dispensation, have left us pointed testimony as to the identity and location of Cumorah or Ramah. (*Doctrines of Salvation,* 3:232–41).[21]

Gordon Hinckley, the current LDS Prophet, writing on the Restoration of the Church, states that after locating the Golden Plates, Joseph Smith translated the *Book of Mormon* into English.

> On the 6th of April, 1830, six men came together and Joseph Smith was declared a prophet, an apostle of Jesus Christ, and has been regarded since that time as the Prophet.[22]

Joseph Smith had established the Restoration of the Kingdom of God, the Restoration of the Gospel, and the Restoration of the Church. (On the Mormon doctrine of Restoration, see pp. 17–21.) Brigham Young so revered Joseph Smith that he once claimed that "the period will come when the people will be willing to adopt Joseph Smith as their prophet, seer and revelator and God!" (*Journal of Wilford Woodruff*, 11 Dec. 1869).

WAS JOSEPH SMITH A PROPHET?

Before we briefly discuss the Mormon claim of a Restored Church, we must first look at the single authority figure who was able, according to LDS teaching, to bring about a full Restoration of the Church of Christ. As we've seen, Joseph Smith proclaimed himself to be a Prophet of God. He claimed to be able to decipher "Reformed Egyptian" engravings on the Golden Plates, which he then translated into the *Book of Mormon*. But how do we know he was a Prophet? Can we take his word for it? We must have an objective test to determine whether the revelations he gave and the works that he delivered to the LDS Church are true. If Joseph Smith was a false prophet, none of the claims of the Mormon Church have any foundation in truth.

When is a Prophet actually speaking for God and when is a Prophet speaking for himself? Can a phrase that is spoken by a man be divine? Ought we to take all of the statements by a self-proclaimed Prophet as inspired? Can a Prophet be wrong or mistaken?

The Old Testament has much to say about testing false prophets. Deuteronomy teaches that if a prophet's revelation does not come to pass, he is a false prophet:

> And if thou say in thine heart, How shall we know the word which the LORD hath not spoken? When a prophet speaketh in the name of the LORD, if the thing follow not, nor come to pass, that is the thing which the LORD hath not spoken, but the prophet hath spoken it presumptuously: thou shalt not be afraid of him. (Deut. 18:21–22)

The sixth Mormon Prophet, Joseph Fielding Smith, similarly claimed that if a man acts without God, then error is sure to follow:

> No man, in and of himself, without the aid of the Spirit of God and the direction of revelation, can found a religion, or promulgate a body of doctrine, in all particulars in harmony with revealed truth. If he has not the inspiration of the Lord and the direction of messengers from his presence, he will not comprehend the truth, and therefore such truth as he teaches will be hopelessly mixed with error.[23]

Some Mormons may say, when confronted with a false prophecy by one of their leaders, that the prophecy didn't come to pass exactly as it was written. They may also say that the Prophet was sharing an opinion, or even that he made a mistake (e.g., Brigham Young made a mistake when he claimed that Adam was God and was the actual Father of Jesus, as will be discussed in a later chapter). However, when a Prophet makes a "Thus saith the Lord" type of statement, that Prophet is claiming that he is speaking directly for God. If the statement is untrue, it is not simply bad judgment; it is a false prophecy of a false prophet.

> We must have an *objective* way to *test* whether Joseph Smith was really a prophet. Since there are dozens of people who claim to be a prophet of God, there must be some way to distinguish between true and false prophets. . . . False prophecies are not mistakes. We all make mistakes but most of us never claimed to be a prophet of God who speaks inspired revelations. To equate false prophecies with mistakes is like equating apples and shoestrings. There is no logical connection.[24]

> If his [Joseph Smith's] claims to a divine appointment be false, forming as they do the foundation of the Church in this the last dispensation, the superstructure cannot be stable.[25]

If we are to know whether a statement is from God, we must have an objective means to discover the Truth. We are commanded in the Bible to seek the Truth, not only with our hearts, but by examining events, statements, or any-

thing else that bears on the validity of the teachings of men. All teachings must be weighed against the witness of Scripture.

What exactly does the Mormon Church consider acceptable to use as Scripture? Are the Prophets from the Church of Jesus Christ of Latter-day Saints viewed as giving "inspired" guidance?

> The prophecies from *Doctrine and Covenants* come from an inspired book of the Mormons. Each inspired revelation is dated and numbered. They usually begin by saying, Thus says the Lord. Thus they are *not* mere opinions or guesses made by Smith but inspired prophecies.[26]

> We believe that God is as willing today as He ever has been to reveal His mind and will to man, and that He does so through His appointed servants—prophets, seers, and revelators—invested through ordination with the authority of the Holy Priesthood.[27]

Some Mormons, when confronted with errors of previous LDS Prophets, may say that new Prophets take precedence over earlier Prophets, and that any mistakes are only human misunderstandings. That would be nice if it worked. The issue is not which Prophet takes precedence or which prophecy of God should apply to the LDS Church today. The main point of those who are critical of the Mormon Church is that the foundation of the Mormon Church is built on a plethora of errors, false prophecies, and unbiblical doctrines.

> If the words of the prophet are of equal validity to the written word, Mormons cannot be so quick to distance themselves from past teachings. If both are inspired, there should be no contradiction.[28]

> A prophet is a man called by God to be his representative on earth. When a prophet speaks for God, it is as if God were speaking. . . . [He] teaches truth and interprets the word of God. We should follow his inspired teachings completely. We should not choose to follow part of his inspired counsel and discard that which is unpleasant or difficult.[29]

Joseph Smith is accepted by the Church of Jesus Christ of Latter-day Saints as a Prophet. He translated the *Book of Mormon,* received revelations, which are shared in *Doctrine and Covenants* and translated the *Pearl of Great Price.* Together with the King James Version of the Bible, these books are considered, by the LDS, to be the Standard Works and Scriptures of God. If the teachings found in the Standard Works of the Mormon Church are found to be false, then great caution must be used in accepting anything from Joseph Smith or any other Prophet from the LDS community.

DOES THE TRUE CHURCH NEED TO BE RESTORED?

If in the nineteenth century our Lord Christ needed to restore the Church to His true Gospel through Joseph Smith, then the Christian Church has not been correct in its understanding of the Gospel for almost two thousand years. If the Restoration ushered in by Smith was not needed,

however, then the very foundation of the Church of Jesus Christ of Latter-day Saints is invalid, and the LDS Church itself is not necessary to the Kingdom of God.

Many Mormon followers believe that the Restoration of the Gospel and the Restoration of the authority of their Aaronic and Melchizedek Priesthoods were completed in the revelations of God to Joseph Smith. This Restoration is the basis for the LDS Priesthood authority. According to the LDS Church, without a full Restoration no Church can claim to be the true Church of Christ.

LDS Prophets have claimed that the Restoration of the true Christian Church was completed in the work of the Prophet Joseph Smith. Their belief is that the authority of the true Church of Jesus Christ was lost after the Apostolic Age, and a Great Apostasy fell on the face of Christianity, which led to a corruption of the truths of Scripture. There are some within the Mormon Church, however, who adamantly deny that the full Restoration of the Church took place in Joseph Smith's time and state that it will be complete only when Christ returns. But LDS leaders have taught that the Restoration of the Church was fully accomplished by Joseph Smith.

While speaking of the establishment of the Church of Jesus Christ of Latter-day Saints as the Restored Church, Joseph Fielding Smith, a Prophet of the Church, stated that the Restoration began with Joseph Smith:

> Following the raising of this *ensign*, the Lord sent forth his elders clothed with the priesthood and with power and authority, among the nations of the earth, bearing witness unto all peoples of the restoration of his Church, and calling upon the chil-

> dren of men to repent and receive the gospel; for now it was being preached in all the world as a witness before the end should come, that is, the end of the reign of wickedness and the establishment of the millennial reign of peace. The elders went forth as they were commanded, and are still preaching the gospel and gathering out from the nations the seed of Israel unto whom the promise was made.[30]

The Prophet Joseph Fielding Smith went on to say that Joseph Smith was unique in his announcement that a Restoration of the Church has taken place:

> No one else, but Joseph Smith, has ever made the claim that this restoration and setting up of the kingdom (i.e., Church of Jesus Christ) has ever been revealed. Yet all indications point to the fact that the predicted signs of the approach of the second coming of our Lord are here. Surely the preparatory work of that coming must precede it. The restored unadulterated gospel must be here. Prophets who can receive revelation and who possess heavenly powers must be here.[31]

Other LDS Prophets have also made similar claims. Harold B. Lee finds the LDS Church's claim to be quite a point of departure from other churches:

> The Church of Jesus Christ of Latter-day Saints is the one church that declares that the gospel was upon the earth from the days of Adam, and today it

> is but a restoration of that early church. I think no other church makes such a claim.[32]

Spencer W. Kimball, another Mormon Prophet, affirms that the Restoration occurred with the founding of the LDS Church:

> Less than a year after the restoration of the Church of Jesus Christ, the Redeemer spoke concerning the ugly sin of infidelity and lustfulness and the conditions for receiving forgiveness.[33]

Finally, Ezra Taft Benson, the thirteenth Prophet of the LDS Church, said that the true Church was restored through Joseph Smith:

> After the restoration of His Church in modern times, Jesus Christ named His Church. With impeccable logic, He inquired of a former generation, How be it my church save it be called in my name? . . . if it be called in the name of a man then it be the church of a man.[34]

We have labored the point in order to demonstrate the primary accusation of Mormons against the whole of Christianity: They teach that not since the time of the Apostles has there been a true Church that contains the true Gospel. This is an incredible claim. This means that since around the time the Apostle John died, every individual who has placed faith in Christ for personal salvation has taken part in the Great Apostasy and rejected the "true" LDS Gospel.

Billy Graham, Martin Luther, Charles Swindoll, John Hus, Augustine, Adoniram Judson, Charles Spurgeon, John Calvin, George Whitefield. All of these men are recognized as Christian leaders and teachers who have proclaimed the Gospel to vast numbers of people with exhortations to believe in Christ. According to Mormon claims, all of these men were misled. Mormons teach that not only have Christians not had authority to speak in the name of God, and not only have Christians been believing a corrupted Gospel, but also there has been no true Church in all of Christianity. The members of the LDS Church are taught that since the death of the last New Testament Apostle, the Truth was lost until it was restored as the "Church of Jesus Christ of Latter-day Saints" in 1830.

As Christian apologists John Ankerberg and John Weldon note, the Mormon Church is in a dilemma regarding its claim of the Restoration of the Church. In Matthew 16:18, Jesus taught that Hell would not prevail against His Church. But if Joseph Smith restored the Gospel, the authority of Priesthood, and the Church, then Christ's claims were false. If Joseph Smith did indeed restore the true Church, then Hell did prevail against Christ's true Church in what Mormons call the Great Apostasy.[35]

It should be apparent that the claims of Joseph Smith and other Mormons concerning the Restoration must be accepted if the LDS wish to propagate their beliefs. If there were no need for a Restoration, all the beliefs at the foundation of Mormonism would be irrelevant.

2

THE STANDARD WORKS

Many statements have been made by authorities within the LDS Church regarding the validity of the *Book of Mormon* as containing the Gospel. But what exactly should be accepted as divinely inspired? What should be accepted as coming from God? Consider, for instance, that the *Pearl of Great Price,* a sacred Mormon text, claims that the *Book of Mormon* contains the complete Gospel of salvation. But if Joseph Smith wrote both the *Book of Mormon* and *Pearl of Great Price* from his own imagination, are we able to accept one as a proof for the other?

We must go to the Old and New Testaments of the Bible and see if what Joseph Smith delivered is in fact in harmony with God's revealed Word. What is most striking is the circular validation of various Mormon texts (i.e., the *Book of Mormon* validates the *Pearl of Great Price,* which validates *Doctrine and Covenants,* and so on). We are told, for example, regarding the *Book of Mormon:*

> And [God] gave him power from on high, by the means which were before prepared, to translate the Book of Mormon; Which contains a record of a fallen people, and the fulness of the gospel of Jesus Christ to the Gentiles and to the Jews also.[1]

The Eighth Article of Faith, found at the end of the *Pearl of Great Price,* states the official LDS position on the authority of the Bible as compared to the *Book of Mormon:*

> We believe the Bible to be the word of God as far as it is translated correctly; we also believe the Book of Mormon to be the Word of God.[2]

In like manner, *Doctrine and Covenants,* another sacred text of the Mormon Church, claims not only that the *Book of Mormon* contains the full Gospel, but that the Bible contains the fullness of the Gospel as well:

> And again, the elders, priests and teachers of this church shall teach the principles of my gospel, which are in the Bible and Book of Mormon, in the which is the fulness of the gospel.[3]

Later on, *Doctrine and Covenants* demonstrates the exalted view of Joseph Smith that is commonly shared within the Mormon Church. Indeed, Joseph Smith and the *Book of Mormon* are central to the LDS belief system:

> Joseph Smith, the Prophet and Seer of the Lord, has done more, save Jesus only, for the salvation of men in this world, than any other man that ever lived in

> it. In the short space of twenty years, he has brought forth the Book of Mormon, which he translated by the gift and power of God, and has been the means of publishing it on two continents; has sent the fulness of the everlasting gospel, which it contained, to the four quarters of the earth.[4]

Joseph Smith, the founder of Mormonism, understood the centrality of the *Book of Mormon* to this new religion. Read very carefully, from the *History of the Church,* what he had to say about the *Book of Mormon,* which he translated from the Golden Plates. Additionally, note that the attack on the Gospel and Christianity began in the early years of Smith's preaching:

> I [Joseph Smith] told the brethren that the Book of Mormon was the most correct of any book on earth, and the keystone of our religion, and a man would get nearer to God by abiding by its precepts, than by any other book.[5]

During his ministry Joseph Smith claimed to have received many revelations from God and published them in the *Book of Commandments*. After many revisions a new edition was printed in 1835 under the title *Doctrine and Covenants*.[6] These revelations underwent significant changes and alterations between the *first* two editions. If the revelations were truly from God, why should any editing or revision be made?

The *Book of Mormon* and *Doctrine and Covenants* are not the only sacred texts for the LDS Church. A third text, *Pearl of Great Price,* was printed as a whole in 1851. The first section of the *Pearl of Great Price* is the Book of Moses, which includes a creation account revealed by Joseph Smith.

Some of the "sacred" texts have caused the Mormon Church embarrassment. Consider the following example. In 1842, Joseph Smith published what he called the Book of Abraham. This comprises the second section of the current edition of the *Pearl of Great Price.* The original form of this document came from papyri found in Egypt in 1831 by Antonio Sebolo. They were brought to Joseph Smith by Michael H. Chandler in 1835. In the same year, Smith purchased the papyri and numerous mummies from Chandler. Smith then allegedly "translated" the papyri into English by the gift of God.

Smith made the claim that the patriarch Abraham was the actual author of one of the fragments. Since 1912, however, numerous Egyptologists, including some LDS scholars, have studied the papyri and have found them to consist of approximately 87 words from the Egyptian Book of the Dead. The difficulty: Smith claimed to have translated these 87 Egyptian words into the Book of Abraham, an 11-page document containing over 4,000 words. At this rate, each Egyptian hieroglyph would have to translate into an average of 46 English words. In essence, this recent finding demonstrates that Joseph Smith was being fraudulent, with no actual gift *or* ability to translate these hieroglyphics.

The third section of the *Pearl of Great Price* is Smith's "translation" of Matthew 24; the fourth section is the Articles of Faith. The *Book of Mormon, Doctrine and Covenants,* and the *Pearl of Great Price* together make up three of the four Standard Works accepted as authoritative for guidance and teaching in Mormon life. The LDS Church also recognizes the Old and New Testaments as a sacred text, but only where the Bible does not contradict Mormon teachings.

While the Bible is accepted as God's Word, the Mormon Apostle Orson Pratt said that

> so far as the uninspired translators and the people are concerned, NO PART of the Bible can, with certainty, be known by them to be the word of God.[7]

Even though many of the Mormon leaders have reflected this viewpoint, the King James Version is used as an authoritative guide to Truth within the LDS Church.

Table 2.1. The Standard Works

1. *Book of Mormon*
2. *Doctrine and Covenants*
3. *Pearl of Great Price*
4. King James Version of the Bible

The Holy Bible

Although the Mormon Church officially recognizes the books that are found in the Old and New Testaments excluding the Apocrypha, many Mormons have been taught that the Old and New Testaments used by other groups are not on par with the Scriptures that Joseph Smith translated. Told that they are the true followers of Jesus Christ, Mormons are presented with a dilemma: How can we accept the Bible, but reject the other groups that claim to believe it? The solution was briefly presented in our earlier discussion on the Restoration of the Church (pp. 17–20). A universal apostasy must have occurred.

The common claim is that early in the history of the Christian Church there was a Great Apostasy; as a result, the Scripture texts were corrupted. Joseph Smith's Restoration of the Church was an attempt to correct this apostasy. Among the corrective measures was that the LDS Church uses the King James Version of the Bible together with a few select passages translated by Joseph Smith inserted at the end of the New Testament.

In the attempt to validate the claim that biblical Truth is found only in the Mormon Church, the LDS commit a grave error: the Mormon Church uses the same translation of the Bible that they criticize others for using. I have had many discussions with LDS Church members regarding doctrines on which we disagree. A common reply is, "Of course you disagree. You're using a corrupted version of the Bible." However, the Mormon Church uses the same version of the Bible that it criticizes many non-Mormons for using; it is the same "corrupted" text. This prompts us to ask whether the LDS believe that their version of the Bible may contain human errors. They believe it does.

Let us consider a few statements of the official LDS Church position regarding the nature of the Bible and the validity and accuracy of the King James Version:

> And again, the elders, priests, and teachers of the church shall teach the principles of my gospel, which are in the Bible.[8]

> These books are called the standard works of the Church. The inspired words of our living prophets are also accepted as scripture.[9]

> The Bible, Book of Mormon, Doctrine and Covenants, and the Pearl of Great Price, including the

> Articles of Faith, have been received by the vote of the Church in general conference assembled as the standard works of the Church.[10]

Yet, while the LDS claim to uphold the Bible, they simultaneously discredit and disavow the Bible's content in favor of the *Book of Mormon:*[11]

> Ignorant translators, careless transcribers, or designing and corrupt priests have committed many errors.[12]

> We believe the Bible to be the word of God *as far as it is translated correctly;* we also believe the Book of Mormon to be the Word of God.[13]

Other LDS leaders have made similar assertions in agreement with the official LDS teachings cited above.[14]

Thus any section of the Bible that seems to contradict or disprove any LDS teaching can be safely ignored by the LDS as having been "translated incorrectly." At the same time, they claim to believe in the Bible so as not to cast suspicion on their faith by discarding the Bible completely.[15]

Many members of the LDS Church will tell those outside their fellowship that the Bible that they are using was corrupted in the Great Apostasy. These same LDS members have been told that the Bible, the *Book of Mormon, Doctrine and Covenants,* and the *Pearl of Great Price* contain the complete Gospel. The problem here is that the same King James Version of the Bible that is thought to be "corrupted" has been accepted by the Church as containing the true Gospel. The LDS Church cannot logically criticize the non-Mormon for using a corrupted Bible if it uses the same Bible.

This extremely common line of attack taken by the Mormon missionary and the regular LDS member is highly inconsistent.

The LDS Church prints, distributes, and recommends the King James Version as a fully reliable explanation of the Gospel. Many a Mormon will say, however, that it does contain the Gospel, but not the full and restored Gospel as in the *Book of Mormon*. Ask that person: What is it in the *Book of Mormon* that is not in the Old or New Testament but is necessary for my salvation?

THE *BOOK OF MORMON*

The *Book of Mormon* comprises a variety of writings: 1 Nephi, 2 Nephi, Jacob, Enos, Jarom, Omni, Words of Mormon, Mosiah, Alma, Helaman, 3 Nephi, 4 Nephi, Mormon, Ether, and Moroni.

We have already seen ample evidence to demonstrate that these works are considered authoritative by the LDS Church. The following selection provides not only an excellent characterization of the importance of the *Book of Mormon* to all LDS members, but also a wonderful demonstration of the teaching that the *Book of Mormon* contains the complete Gospel message:

> It [the *Book of Mormon*] contains the fulness of the everlasting gospel. . . . these records preserved a true knowledge of God, of the mission and ministry of his Son, and of the doctrines and ordinances of salvation. . . . Take away the Book of Mormon and the revelations, and where is our religion? We have none. . . . The work [*Book of Mormon*] is true.[16]

Table 2.2. *Book of Mormon*

1 Nephi	Omni	3 Nephi
2 Nephi	Words of Mormon	4 Nephi
Jacob	Mosiah	Mormon
Enos	Alma	Ether
Jarom	Helaman	Moroni

What exactly is the Gospel? What is faith? What is salvation? Why should we accept the *Book of Mormon* if it contains nothing that is not included in the Old or New Testament? These can be difficult questions for LDS Church members to answer. It is essential for them to see the lack of need for the *Book of Mormon.* If the Bible contains the true Gospel and is written by dozens of witnesses to God and His Son, why is there need for the *Book of Mormon?*

Doctrine and Covenants

LDS members are to accept the series of revelations in *Doctrine and Covenants* as they would the Bible or the *Book of Mormon. Doctrine and Covenants,* the third set of writings considered to be divinely inspired, is a collection of prophecies spanning revelations from 1823 until 1978. It, too, is regarded as presenting the full Gospel:

> And whatsoever they shall speak when moved upon by the Holy Ghost shall be scripture, shall be the will of the Lord, shall be the mind of the Lord, shall be the word of the Lord, shall be the voice of the Lord, and the power of God unto salvation.[17]

> It is a selection of revelations which contain doctrines and commandments covering every phase of salvation, which, if we will follow them, will direct us to the celestial kingdom.[18]

TABLE 2.3. *PEARL OF GREAT PRICE*

MOSES
ABRAHAM
GOSPEL OF MATTHEW (JOSEPH SMITH'S TRANSLATION)
BRIEF HISTORY OF JOSEPH SMITH
ARTICLES OF FAITH

PEARL OF GREAT PRICE

The *Pearl of Great Price* comprises the book of Moses, the book of Abraham, Joseph Smith's translation of the Gospel of Matthew, a short history of Joseph Smith, and the Articles of Faith. (The section Articles of Faith should not be confused with the book of the same title by James Talmage.) As one of the Standard Works, the *Pearl of Great Price* is regarded as fully authoritative:

> This expression, Pearl of Great Price, has been adopted as the title of a volume of latter-day scripture, a volume containing a choice selection of the revelations, translations, and narrations of the Prophet Joseph Smith.[19]

> The Articles of Faith have been accepted by the people as an authoritative exposition; and on October 6, 1890, the Latter-day Saints, in general conference

assembled, readopted the Articles as a guide in faith and conduct.[20]

The four sacred texts of the Mormon Church, sometimes called the Standard Works, are regarded as given by God to the people of the Church of Jesus Christ of Latter-day Saints. Officially accepted as divine works, the Bible, the *Book of Mormon, Doctrine and Covenants,* and *Pearl of Great Price* are trusted on all matters of concern to the LDS community.

3

THE MORMON GOSPEL

For the Christian, the Gospel is quite simple. The eternal God, revealed as the Trinity, created all things. He created Adam and Eve in the Garden. Our first parents sinned. Because of their sin, there is enmity between God and man. Jesus Christ was crucified on the cross and received the punishment due for sin on behalf of all who believe in Him. The Holy Spirit works to make alive those who are dead in sin. Those who believe in Him will one day enter His presence and will remain there for all eternity. Those who do not believe in Him will be sentenced to eternal punishment.

The LDS version of salvation, exaltation, and eternal progression is a little more involved. The God of Mormonism was once a man like us. He lived on His own planet and had a god over Him (and so on into eternity past). Through perfect obedience, He achieved exaltation to godhood. He had a wife and had millions of spirit-children with her. Jesus and Lucifer were brothers who fought over the best way to deal with Earth and all who inhabited it. Lucifer

and his friends rebelled and were cast out of Heaven. Jesus was awarded the office of Savior for Earth. The rest of us who lived in the "pre-existence" have come to Earth in order to earn our exaltation and become gods like the God of the Bible. We will have wives and spirit-children just as God does if we are perfect enough in this life to gain that privilege. We will gain in wisdom just as God does. One day we will be as powerful as He is. Depending on how obedient we are, we will ultimately end up in one of three eternal Kingdoms: the Telestial Kingdom, the Terrestrial Kingdom, and, for the most faithful Mormons, the Celestial Kingdom (which is where the LDS believe God is). The great majority of those who reject the *Book of Mormon* or have never heard of it will one day end up in the lowest Kingdom, the Telestial Kingdom. Those who are given over to satanic principles will stay in outer darkness with Satan and the other rebellious spirits forever.

What Is the Gospel?

In this chapter, we will look at the teaching of the Bible on the subject of the Gospel. We will look at the nature of the Gospel and the purpose of the Gospel as described by Scripture. If the Gospel is what the LDS teach, we should expect to find more than ample evidence for the Gospel as a plan or tool to bring mankind to exaltation to godhood through obedience and good works. If the orthodox Christian teaching is correct, however, we should find that there is only one God, that our being accounted righteous is not based on our good works, and that faith in Christ frees us from the wrath of God and the power of sin.

According to Scripture, the wrath of God is revealed against all who are unrighteous (Rom. 1:18). We all have sinned and fallen short of the glory of God (Rom. 3:23) and are therefore under the curse of God for our sin.

How is this relationship between God and man restored? The Apostle Paul speaks of this at great length in the New Testament book of Romans. In particular, if we look at Romans 3:20–22, we are instructed that "by the deeds of the law there shall no flesh be justified." Instead, the "righteousness of God without the law is manifested . . . even the righteousness of God which is by faith of Jesus Christ unto all and upon all them that believe."[1]

Because all have sinned, God "hath set forth [Christ] to be a propitiation through faith in his blood, to declare his righteousness for the remission of sins" of mankind (3:25). Christ is the "appeasement of wrath" for all who believe in His death, burial, and resurrection. God has declared that Christ's work is righteous and a perfect atonement for the forgiveness of our sins if we believe in Christ.

Can we boast in this righteousness of Christ? No, Paul argues, all boasting is excluded by the law of faith. This is not some law of works by which we satisfy the righteousness of God, but of faith in the righteous work of Christ that we are "justified by faith without the deeds of the law" (vv. 27–28).

Paul continues his account of faith in Christ as the ground of our salvation by describing the faith of Abraham in the fourth chapter of Romans. Abraham was not justified by works; if he had been, he would have received glory and had reason to boast, but not before God. But "Abraham believed God, and it was counted unto him for righteousness" (Gal. 3:6). If the salvation offered by God were by works, any works, it would not be according to grace, but would be a reward or a debt paid by God for righteousness earned (4:2–4). On the other hand, the faith of those who do not work but believe in Christ, who justifies the sinner, is counted as righteousness.

John 3:18 stands as a warning to those who reject the righteousness of Christ. All who do not believe "in the name of the only begotten Son of God" will be condemned.

"That's fine," someone might say, "but what are we supposed to believe in for salvation?" The Apostle Paul clarifies the Gospel of Christ with these words:

> Moreover, brethren, I declare unto you the gospel which I preached unto you, which also ye have received, and wherein ye stand; By which also ye are saved, if ye keep in memory what I preached unto you, unless ye have believed in vain. For I delivered unto you first of all that which I also received, how that Christ died for our sins according to the scriptures; And that he was buried, and that he rose again the third day according to the scriptures: And that he was seen of Cephas, then of the twelve: After that, he was seen of above five hundred brethren at once; of whom the greater part remain unto this present, but some are fallen asleep. After that, he was seen of James; then of all the apostles. And last of all he was seen of me also, as of one born out of due time. For I am the least of the apostles, that am not meet to be called an apostle, because I persecuted the church of God. But by the grace of God I am what I am: and his grace which was bestowed upon me was not in vain; but I laboured more abun-

> dantly than they all: yet not I, but the grace of God which was with me. Therefore whether it were I or they, so we preach, and so ye believed. (1 Cor. 15:1–11)

In 1 Corinthians 15:1–2 and 11, the Apostle Paul defines the Gospel of Christ by first reminding the Church at Corinth that the Gospel is firmly founded in the received apostolic tradition. This passage does not set out to define the Gospel of Christ as some new revelation; rather, it sets out to remind the Corinthians that the Gospel has already been delivered to them.

In verses 3–4, Paul repeats the content of the apostolic tradition that was given to him. The Corinthians had apparently forgotten the essential character and mission of Christ. Christ was raised from the dead according to the Scriptures and according to Paul's preaching and the message in which the Corinthians had already believed. Here Paul makes plain that the atonement for sins through the death of Christ is based on His resurrection; later in the text he argues that to deny the bodily resurrection of believers is to deny the resurrection of Christ and ultimately the atonement itself.

There is much more material in this passage that can be commented on, but we will focus upon the definition and meaning of the Apostolic Gospel message. Note the outline that the Apostle Paul presents at the start—the Gospel is:

1. That which he had preached to the Corinthians already.
2. That which they had already heard.
3. That by which they were saved.

Paul explains that the Gospel he is declaring is that which the Corinthians have already received. The Gospel message is "that Christ died for our sins according to the scriptures, And that he was buried, and that he rose again the third day according to the scriptures," and that Christ was seen by many witnesses shortly after. Paul names Cephas, the Twelve, five hundred brethren, James, and finally himself as witnesses of the resurrection of Christ.

In verse 3, Paul reminds the Corinthians that Scripture itself testifies to the death of Christ for our sins. Matthew 27:35–46, for example, indicates that the words of the Prophet were fulfilled at the crucifixion. This is a reference to Psalm 22:1–18. Jesus Himself quoted Psalm 22:1 before He yielded up His Spirit. Christ died according to the Scriptures of the Old Testament. Paul had to remind the Corinthians that the Old Testament contained the Gospel.

In verse 4 Paul then teaches that according to the Scriptures, Christ's resurrection is also an essential part of the Gospel. We see the original prophecy in Psalm 16:9–11:

> Therefore my heart is glad, and my glory rejoiceth: my flesh also shall rest in hope. For thou wilt not leave my soul in hell; neither wilt thou suffer thine Holy One to see corruption. Thou wilt shew me the path of life: in thy presence is fulness of joy; at thy right hand there are pleasures for evermore.

This passage was cited by Peter in Acts 2:25–28 as a reference to Christ's resurrection. Additionally, when Paul was in Antioch of Pisidia, he told his audience that Christ was raised from the dead according to the prophecy of Psalm 16:10 (cf. Acts 13:35).

These Scriptures indicate the nature of the Gospel as defined by the Apostles, within the community of faith, and according to the testimony of the Old Testament. Paul's message to the Corinthians defines the heart of the Gospel. It has been preached, taught, and remembered among the contemporaries of the New Testament witnesses.

Paul also speaks of the saving nature of the Gospel through Christ's death in Colossians 1:19–23:

> For it pleased the Father that in him should all fulness dwell; And, having made peace through the blood of his cross, by him to reconcile all things unto himself; by him, I say, whether they be things in earth, or things in heaven. And you, that were sometime alienated and enemies in your mind by wicked works, yet now hath he reconciled in the body of his flesh through death, to present you holy and unblameable and unreproveable in his sight: If ye continue in the faith grounded and settled, and be not moved away from the hope of the gospel, which ye have heard, and which was preached to every creature which is under heaven; whereof I Paul am made a minister.

The Apostle makes it clear that according to the Gospel of Christ we who were formerly enemies of God have been reconciled to the Father through the death of Christ. Christ presents us as "unblameable" and "unreproveable" in the Father's sight when we believe and trust in Him alone to save us.

Simply put, the Gospel that was declared by Paul is the Apostolic Gospel, the Gospel of Christ in which we have

believed. It is the Gospel that was handed down to the Corinthians through the Apostles themselves. It is the Gospel that has been handed down to us through the Scriptures. We who were once enemies of God are now justified by faith in His Son Jesus Christ, who bore our sins on the cross.

What Saith the Prophets of the Latter-day Saints?

Although he was not a Prophet of the LDS Church, James E. Talmage was a leader within that community for many years and highly regarded for his contributions to that belief system. In his work *Articles of Faith* he comments:

> It is alike impossible for any spirit, in the flesh or disembodied, to obtain promise of eternal glory except on condition of obedience to the laws and ordinances of the Gospel. And, as baptism is essential to the salvation of the living, it is likewise indispensable to the dead.[2]

The Apostle Paul was a self-confessed murderer (1 Cor. 15:9; Acts 7:54–8:3). If James Talmage is correct, Paul could not have simply called upon his faith in Christ for deliverance from his sins. In order to be saved, Paul would have had to be perfectly obedient to the "laws and ordinances of the Gospel."[3] Similarly, in his comments on "justification by faith alone," Talmage says:

> Yet in spite of the plain word of God, dogmas of men have been promulgated to the effect that by faith alone may salvation be attained, and that a

> wordy profession of belief shall open the doors of heaven to the sinner.[4]

Elsewhere he adds:

> The Sectarian Dogma of Justification by Faith Alone has exercised an influence for evil.[5]

George Q. Cannon, another respected LDS figure, was likewise very clear about what is required for salvation:

> Baptism is . . . only one of the rounds in the Gospel ladder which reaches from the depth of the degradation into which poor humanity has fallen to the Celestial Kingdom of God. But the poor prisoner who wishes to escape from his dungeon must take step after step up the ladder until he reaches the top and can breathe once more the free air of heaven, or he will not be benefited; the ladder is his means for attaining the desired end—liberty. The Gospel is our means of gaining our important end—salvation. But we must obey every principle, or we cannot be saved; we must take every step up the ladder, or we cannot get into the Celestial Kingdom. The moment we set bounds to our faith and works, that moment our salvation ceases.[6]

It may not be entirely accurate to claim that the LDS believe that baptism by itself gains an individual salvation, but it is clear that baptism is regarded as a necessary work to obtain salvation. It is to the LDS a rung in the ladder that man must climb by his own effort. Wilford Woodruff once

said that the good works we do in this life "are not for the exaltation of the Almighty, but they are for us," in order that we might ascend and become gods.[7]

Some might argue that the quotations of George Q. Cannon and James Talmage cannot be considered representative of the official teaching of the Latter-day Saints, because they were not Prophets. We should turn then to one who was. Joseph F. Smith (who is to be distinguished from Joseph Smith and Joseph Fielding Smith), the sixth President (Prophet) of the LDS Church, had this to say about the role of faith in salvation:

> The fulness of the everlasting gospel was preached, through which we will be exalted, for there is no exaltation except through obedience to law. *Every blessing, privilege, glory, or exaltation is obtained only through obedience to the law upon which the same is promised. If we will abide by the law, we shall receive the reward; but we can receive it on no other ground.* Then let us rejoice in the truth, in the restoration of the Priesthood—that power delegated to man, by virtue of which the Lord sanctions in the heavens what man does upon the earth. The Lord has taught us the *ordinances of the gospel by which we may perfect our exaltation in his kingdom*. We are not living as the heathen, without law; that which is necessary for our exaltation has been revealed. Our duty, therefore, is to obey the laws; then we shall receive our reward.[8] (emphasis added)

This LDS Prophet flatly denies the orthodox Christian and biblical doctrine of justification by faith alone. Not only does Joseph F. Smith claim that faith in Christ is not sufficient to save a person, he mocks the teaching of justification by faith in Christ by calling it "unscriptural"; "it is unreasonable, it is untrue, and it will not avail any man, no matter by whom this idea may be advocated; it will prove an utter failure unto men."[9]

In view of Paul's definition of the Gospel of salvation that was preached to the Corinthians, how can we not hold suspect the teachings of the LDS Prophet Joseph F. Smith? The Apostle Paul himself in Galatians 1:6–12 warns against such a denial of the essence of the Gospel. Paul was very anxious to direct the Galatians away from those who wanted to "pervert" the Gospel of Christ. He argued that if anyone, even an angel, preached anything contrary to the Gospel, such a preacher of a false gospel was damned (anathema). Paul's Gospel was not according to any man, but was revealed directly by God. Those who oppose or alter that Gospel are to be accursed.

Elsewhere, LDS Prophet Joseph F. Smith explains the role of baptism in the ladder of salvation:

> That change comes today to every son and daughter of God who repents of his or her sins, who humble themselves before the Lord, and who seek forgiveness and remission of sin by baptism by immersion, by one having authority to administer this sacred ordinance of the gospel of Jesus Christ.
>
> THE NECESSITY OF BAPTISM . . . The Savior said to Nicodemus, "Except a man be born again, he cannot see the kingdom of God," and that is true today. A man must be born from ignorance into truth, today, before he can expect to see any difference between a Latter-day Saint and another not of

> the faith. If he is not so born, he is more blind than the one whom Christ healed, for having eyes he sees not, and having ears, hears not. Is there any difference between the baptized and the unbaptized man? All the difference in the world, I tell you, but it is only discernible through the Spirit. It is a vast difference too great for one not in possession of the Spirit to comprehend. Take two men, they may be equals in point of goodness, they may be equally moral, charitable, honest and just, but one is baptized and the other is not. There is a mighty difference between them, for one is the son of God *redeemed by compliance with his laws,* and the other remains in darkness.[10] (emphasis added)

This last paragraph is especially alarming. To the LDS Prophet Joseph F. Smith, being "born again" meant that a person must be baptized to be "redeemed by compliance with his [God's] laws." Redemption, it is claimed, is actually accomplished by obedience to laws!

But is this the meaning of John 3:1–18? Nicodemus comes to Jesus in the middle of the night and says that he knows that Christ is from God. Jesus tells him that unless a man is "born again," he cannot see the Kingdom of God. Nicodemus is not sure what Jesus means and asks how a man can be born when he is already old; how is it possible to enter into the womb a second time to be born? Jesus clarifies what He means by being born again. A man must be born twice: once of the womb, or by the "water of birth," and once by the Spirit of God. Baptism is not mentioned anywhere within the passage. Nor is obedience leading to salvation mentioned anywhere in the passage.

Only upon being born of the Spirit can a man enter the Kingdom of God. Jesus rewords His meaning for Nicodemus again by saying that what is born of flesh, or the first birth, is flesh, but that which is born of the Spirit is spirit.

Just a few verses later, Jesus explains that only by belief in the Son of Man can a person have eternal life. Only by belief in Christ and the renewal of the Spirit of God is a person able to enter into the presence of God for all eternity. All others will be condemned for rejecting Him. Jesus identifies two types of people only: those who believe and have eternal life with the Father, and those who perish forever. There are no multiple levels of Heaven given by Jesus, nor are there levels of obedience listed anywhere in this context.

Thus with Joseph F. Smith's teaching of redemption "by compliance to [God's] laws," we have the most blatant and outright denial of the perfect substitution of Christ for the salvation of man. A man who claimed to be a Prophet of God and spokesman for Christ declared that we are saved by baptism and compliance with the law.

In the Missionary Reference Library, published and distributed by the Church of Jesus Christ of Latter-day Saints, is a book entitled *Gospel Principles.* This book is a collection of short answers and helps on a variety of theological matters. Its topics include "Our Pre-Earth Life with God," "Leaving the Presence of God," "Communication Between God and Man," "Perfecting Our Lives," and "Family Salvation." In chapter 47, "Exaltation," we are told:

> Latter-day Saints are taught that now is the time to fulfill the requirements for exaltation (see Alma 34:32–34). President Joseph Fielding Smith said, "In order to obtain the exaltation we must accept the gospel and all its covenants; and take upon us the obligations which the Lord has offered; and walk in

the light and understanding of the truth; and 'live by every word that proceedeth forth from the mouth of God'" (*Doctrines of Salvation*, 2:43).

There are specific ordinances we must have received to be exalted:

1. We must be baptized and confirmed a member of the Church of Jesus Christ.
2. We must receive the laying on of hands for the gift of the Holy Ghost.
3. We must receive the temple endowment.
4. We must be married for time and all eternity.

In addition to receiving the required ordinances, there are also many laws we have to obey to qualify for exaltation. We must—

1. Love God and worship Him.
2. Have faith in Jesus Christ.
3. Live the law of chastity.
4. Repent of our wrong doings.
5. Pay honest tithes and offerings.
6. Be honest in our dealings with others and with the Lord.
7. Speak the truth always.
8. Obey the Word of Wisdom.[11]
9. Search out our kindred dead and perform the saving ordinances of the Gospel for them.
10. Keep the Sabbath day holy.
11. Attend our Church meetings as regularly as possible to renew our baptismal covenants. This is done as we partake of the sacrament.[12]

12. Love and strengthen our family members in the ways of the Lord.

13. Have family and individual prayers every day.

14. Honor our parents.

15. Teach the Gospel to others by word and example.

16. Study the Scriptures.

17. Listen to and obey the words of the Prophets of the Lord.

18. Develop true charity in our lives.[13]

In contrast to this we have, once again, the clarifying explanation of the Apostle Paul in Galatians 2:14–16:

> But when I saw that they walked not uprightly according to the truth of the gospel, I said unto Peter before them all, If thou, being a Jew, livest after the manner of Gentiles, and not as do the Jews, why compellest thou the Gentiles to live as do the Jews? We who are Jews by nature, and not sinners of the Gentiles, Knowing that a man is not justified by the works of the law, but by the faith of Jesus Christ, even we have believed in Jesus Christ, that we might be justified by the faith of Christ, and not by the works of the law: for by the works of the law shall no flesh be justified.

Prophet Joseph F. Smith claimed that man is "redeemed by compliance with [God's] laws." In other words, obedience to God's laws will result in salvation. But Paul says, "By the works of the law shall no flesh be justified." There is a difficulty here for the LDS who believe in the prophetic office of Joseph F. Smith and the authority of his office. Does the law redeem us, as the LDS teach, or do we confess with the Apostle of Christ that justification is by faith and not by works of the law?

Some might suggest that this legalistic view of redemption given by Joseph F. Smith is just the opinion of one man. Is it really the official doctrine of the LDS Church? Do any of the other Prophets of the LDS Church believe the same thing? Yes. Aside from Joseph Smith, the founder of the LDS religious system, there is in particular one other name that stands out: Brigham Young. He is considered by the LDS Church to be the second Prophet of their organization. He is also considered to be a Prophet of God in our time.

Prophet Brigham Young, as the President of the Latter-day Saints from 1847 to 1877, made many statements concerning the nature of the Gospel:

> The Gospel of the Son of God that has been revealed is a plan or system of laws and ordinances, by strict obedience to which the people who inhabit this earth are assured that they may return again into the presence of the Father and the Son.[14]

And again:

> Our religion, in common with everything of which God is the Author, is a system of law and order. He has instituted laws and ordinances for the government and benefit of the children of men, to see if they would obey them and prove themselves worthy of eternal life by the law of the celestial worlds. This holy Priesthood that we talk about is a perfect system

> of government. By obedience to these laws we expect to enter the celestial kingdom and to be exalted.[15]

There can be little doubt that followers of the LDS Church are very familiar with this teaching. Brigham Young in numerous other places makes quite plain that salvation is by obedience to the law. The testimony of the true Apostles of Christ who, like Paul, declare that faith in Christ is the way of salvation is rejected in LDS theology and Prophetic pronouncements.

The foundation of the true Gospel is Christ's death, resurrection, and ultimate victory over sin. The Scriptures we have examined are very clear on this matter. Yet the Prophets of the LDS Church are equally clear about the basis of their religion: man's works are the center and focus of redemption.

Not only are works the center of the LDS faith, but so is atonement of sins centered on works. The following may not be practiced today, but the teaching has been repeated by numerous LDS Prophets. What is that teaching? That if your sins cannot be cleansed by baptism, you should be killed! If your neighbor commits a sin that prohibits his exaltation to godhood, you should kill him by the "shedding of his blood."

> This is loving our neighbor as ourselves; if he needs help, help him and if he wants salvation and it is necessary to spill his blood on the earth in order that he might be saved, spill it. . . . that is the way to love mankind.[16]

This teaching of salvation by murder is repeated in several passages of LDS literature.[17] Is this doctrine still practiced? Let's pray not.

The denial of the essential character of the Gospel by LDS leaders is compounded by even more wayward theological propositions. Consider a statement in an official publication of the Church of Jesus Christ of Latter-day Saints:

> The Savior atoned for us by suffering in Gethsemane. . . . In the Garden of Gethsemane, the weight of our sins caused him to feel such agony and heartbreak that he bled from every pore.[18]

Bill McKeever cites another example of this rather bizarre doctrine of the LDS Prophets:

> On page fourteen of his book, *Teachings of Ezra Taft Benson,* the thirteenth president of the LDS Church stated it was in the Garden of Gethsemane that Christ "suffered as only God would suffer, bearing our griefs, carrying our sorrows, being wounded for our transgressions, voluntarily submitting Himself to the iniquity of us all, just as Isaiah prophesied." He further stated on that same page: "It was in Gethsemane that Jesus took on Himself the sins of the world, in Gethsemane that His pain was equivalent to the cumulative burden of all men, in Gethsemane that He descended below all things so that all could repent and come to Him."[19]

Against this rather bizarre proclamation stands 1 Corinthians 1:18, 23, which states that the "cross is to them that perish foolishness; but unto us which are saved it is the power of God. . . . We preach Christ crucified, unto the Jews a stumblingblock, and unto the Greeks foolishness." This is the message that Paul preached. This is the testimony of the Gospel tradition, and this is the truth that the LDS Prophets deny, time and time again. Christ was crucified for our sins and on the cross received the curse that was due to us, according to the testimony of the New Testament:

> Who his own self bare our sins in his own body on the tree, that we, being dead to sins, should live unto righteousness. (1 Peter 2:24)

> Christ hath redeemed us from the curse of the law, being made a curse for us: for it is written, Cursed is every one that hangeth on a tree. (Gal. 3:13)

Ephesians 2:16 states that we are reconciled to God "by the cross." In Colossians 1:20 we are told that Christ has "made peace through the blood of his cross." One chapter later, in verse 14, we learn that the requirements of the law have been taken away by Christ and "nailed" to "the cross." The teaching of Scripture is clear that we are not "redeemed by compliance to [God's] laws," but are redeemed by Christ's satisfaction of the requirements of the law on the cross (not in Gethsemane). All this was accomplished according to the command of God in the law (Deut. 21:22–23).

Jesus, in His act on the cross, completed much more than redemption for those who believe in Him. As noted by John Owen,[20] the "death, blood-shedding, or oblation of Jesus Christ" accomplished:

1. Reconciliation with God "by removing and slaying the enmity that was between him and us" (Rom. 5:10; 2 Cor. 5:18–19; Eph. 2:15–16).

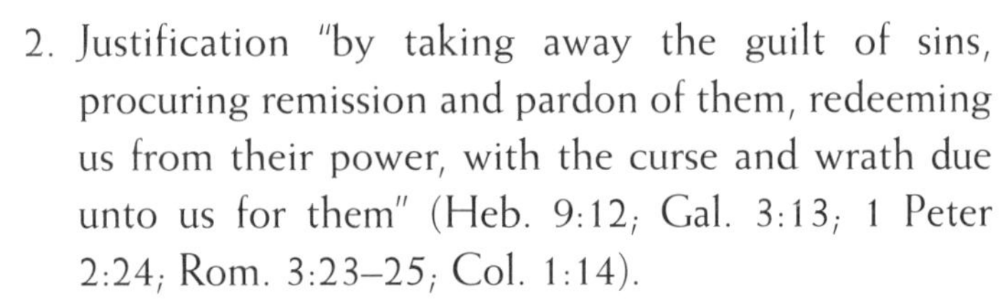

2. Justification "by taking away the guilt of sins, procuring remission and pardon of them, redeeming us from their power, with the curse and wrath due unto us for them" (Heb. 9:12; Gal. 3:13; 1 Peter 2:24; Rom. 3:23–25; Col. 1:14).
3. Sanctification "by the purging away of the uncleanness and pollution of our sins, renewing in us the image of God, and supplying us with the graces of the Spirit of holiness" (Heb. 9:14; 1 John 1:7; Heb. 1:3; Heb. 13:12; Eph. 5:25–27).
4. Adoption "with that evangelical liberty and all those glorious privileges which appertain to the sons of God" (Gal. 4:4–5).

Owen concludes this summary by stating that our "inheritance is a 'purchased possession,'" as recorded in Ephesians 1:14 and Hebrews 9:15, which states that Christ is the "mediator of the new testament" (or New Covenant); through His death "for the redemption of the transgressions that were under the first testament, they which are called might receive the promise of eternal inheritance."

> The sum of all is,—The death and blood-shedding of Jesus Christ hath wrought, and doth effectually procure, for all those that are concerned in it, eternal redemption, consisting in grace here and glory hereafter.[21]

Mormons do not picture final salvation as it is described in Revelation 5:8–14, with the Saints worshipping the Lamb forever and ever. Final salvation for the LDS is "exaltation" to godhood.[22] *Doctrine and Covenants* 132:37, an "inspired" book recognized as binding on all members of the LDS Church as the very Word of God, states the doctrine of "exaltation":

> Abraham received concubines, and they bore him children; and it was accounted unto him for righteousness, because they were given unto him, and he abode in my law; as Isaac also and Jacob did none other things than that which they were commanded; and because they did none other things than that which they were commanded, they have entered into their exaltation, according to the promises, and sit upon thrones, and are not angels but are gods.[23]

The Apostle Paul makes clear in Romans 4:9–12, however, that Abraham was accounted righteous by faith, not by works. In this same section, 4:13–25, the Apostle argues that the promise is according to "faith, that it might be by grace." There is no room for redemption by works, because salvation is not due to obligation, merit, or obedience to the law. Christ was delivered up for our sins and was resurrected so that we may be justified in Him by faith.

Hebrews 10:39 tells us that we "believe [have faith] to the saving of the soul." But what does "faith" mean in this passage? The very next verse tells us. Hebrews 11:1 describes faith as "the substance of things hoped for, the evidence of things not seen." The next few paragraphs list examples of true faith as found throughout the Bible. Abel sacrificed by faith, Enoch was taken away by faith, Noah believed in God by faith, as did Abraham and Sarah. So did Isaac, Jacob, Joseph, Moses, Rahab, Gideon, Barak, Samson, Jephthah, David, Samuel, the Prophets, and many others who were tortured and killed because of their faith.

This passage also tells us that without faith we cannot please God. It is not obedience to the law that makes one righteous, but the "righteousness of faith." Viewed against 1 Corinthians 15, Hebrews 11, and similar passages of the Bible, the theology of the LDS Prophets is a complete denial of the Gospel of Christ, a denial of God's perfect justification, and a denial of His atoning sacrifice for our sins according to faith.

The teaching of eternal progression to godhood plays considerably into the LDS doctrine of salvation (or exaltation). Not only does *Doctrine and Covenants* 132:37 remind us of the Latter-day Saints' doctrine of redemption by obedience to the law, it also asserts that Abraham and his descendants were elevated to godhood expressly by their obedience to the law. According to the Bible, however, there is no plurality of gods and there is no way for man to become like God, despite the declarations of LDS Prophets.[24] Isaiah 44:6–8 states:

> Thus saith the LORD the King of Israel, and his redeemer the LORD of hosts; I am the first, and I am the last; and beside me there is no God. And who, as I, shall call, and shall declare it, and set it in order for me, since I appointed the ancient people? and the things that are coming, and shall come, let them shew unto them. Fear ye not, neither be afraid: have not I told thee from that time, and have declared it? ye are even my witnesses. Is there a God beside me? yea, there is no God; I know not any.

Here we have the unequivocal language of God Himself stating that He is the first and last. There is no god or God before Him. There is no god or God after Him. There is no god or God other than Him at all, anywhere, at any time, or in any way. If God Himself knows of no other God or god, who is Brigham Young to suppose otherwise?

What does the founder of the LDS system, Joseph Smith, say about salvation?

> From what has already been introduced as testimony to prove that no man can be saved without baptism, it will be seen and acknowledged that if there was sin among men, repentance was as necessary at one time or age of the world as another—and that other foundation can no man lay than that is laid, which is Jesus Christ. If, then, Abel was a righteous man he had to become so by keeping the commandments; if Enoch was righteous enough to come into the presence of God, and walk with him, he must have become so by keeping his commandments, and so of every righteous person, whether it was Noah, a preacher of righteousness; Abraham, the father of the faithful; Jacob, the prevailer with God; Moses, the man who wrote of Christ, and brought forth the law by commandment, as a schoolmaster to bring men to Christ, or whether it was Jesus Christ himself.[25]

Here is the founder of the religious system of the Church of Jesus Christ of Latter-day Saints giving his firm position on the doctrine of salvation. Without hesitation, Joseph Smith proclaims that salvation is not possible "without baptism." He proceeds to deny everything that Hebrews 11 establishes: he denies justification by faith alone and the explicit reasoning of Hebrews 11. It seems that early on in the LDS belief system, salvation by works was as alive as it is today.

Of course, members of the Latter-day Saints Church may respond that Joseph Smith did in fact teach salvation by faith apart from works in his *Lectures on Faith*:

> Who cannot see, then, that salvation is the effect of faith? for, as we have previously observed, all the heavenly beings work by this principle; and it is because they are able so to do that they are saved, for nothing but this could save them. And this is the lesson which the God of heaven, by the mouth of all his holy prophets, has been endeavouring to teach to the world.[26]

Here we encounter a difficulty frequently found in LDS teaching. It appears that after the LDS Church was formed, the teachings of its early leaders subtly changed over time and became something entirely different.[27] This makes any attempt to clarify the official Mormon position frustrating and complicated.

It should be remembered that we have clear statements from Joseph Smith, Brigham Young, and others that salvation is by obedience to the law and not exclusively by faith in Christ. Romans 3:28 states, however, that "we conclude that a man is justified by faith without the deeds of the law."[28] This presents a major problem for LDS apologists to overcome in support of their rather flexible theological system.

4

MORMONISM'S DOCTRINE OF GOD

In this chapter we will briefly look at some of the doctrines and teachings about God that are held to be true by the Church of Jesus Christ of Latter-day Saints. We will compare those teachings to the Old and New Testaments as well as to statements from within the LDS Church that are at odds with the official doctrine.

The foundation of any Christian belief is in the Bible, which promotes the teaching of Christ. Anyone wishing to discover whether a "Christian" teaching is the Truth should first turn to the pages of the Old and New Testaments. While comparing doctrines of the LDS Church with the Bible, we will break each topic into two separate sections. The first section will explain current beliefs within Latter-day Saint theology. The second section will use quotations from the Standard Works and the Bible to directly contradict doctrines maintained and taught by the Church of Jesus Christ of Latter-day Saints. This is not to suggest that the

LDS sources are reliable or truthful, but to demonstrate the division within LDS authorities and sources.

How Many Gods Are There?

Throughout the history of the Christian Church there have been attacks from within and without the Church aimed at redefining the Christian understanding of the doctrine of God. Although we will not enter into a study of the history of the heretical teachings concerning the doctrine of God, all serious students should read the formulations of the councils of Nicea and Chalcedon. The events surrounding these two councils shed much light on the dangers of those groups that deny the monotheistic and Trinitarian understanding of God and the revelation of Him in the Old and New Testaments.[1]

THE LDS VIEW

Many LDS members are not aware of the rather distinct doctrine of multiple gods (polytheism). In a personal interview I had with two Mormon missionaries, one gentleman said, "We do not believe that doctrine," only to be refuted by the missionary sitting right beside him. This was rather discouraging. I was asking serious questions about official LDS teaching, and one of the representatives specifically sent to speak to me was not even aware of his own Church's teaching. Maybe he didn't agree with his Church.

Even though Bruce R. McConkie was not a Prophet of the Mormon Church, he was an LDS Apostle for a number of years, and his perspectives are considered the Church's official position on many points of theology:

> . . . Father, Son, and Holy Ghost—comprise the Godhead. As each of these persons is a God, it is evident, from this standpoint alone, that a *plurality of Gods* exists. . . . But in addition there is an infinite number of holy personages, drawn from worlds without number, who have passed on to exaltation and are thus gods . . . and where was there ever a father without first being a son? Whenever did a tree or anything spring into existence without a progenitor?[2]

Statements from *Doctrine and Covenants* have been used by LDS members as common prooftexts to demonstrate the plurality of gods:

> A time to come in the which nothing shall be withheld, whether there be one God or many gods, they shall be manifest.[3]

> According to that which was ordained in the midst of the Council of the Eternal God of all other gods before this world was.[4]

The Mormon Apostle James Talmage made the claim that although Scripture refers to Christ as the Father, it doesn't give any real weight to the idea that He and the Father are equal or share any type of identity with each other. Of course, being an Apostle he apparently was allowed to make such statements within the LDS Church without coming under scrutiny for compromising scriptural teaching. It appears that if Scripture doesn't agree with a personal belief, Scripture is incorrect. Scripture is not the final authority for the LDS theological system. James Talmage summarizes the issue:

> That Jesus Christ or Jehovah is designated in certain scriptures as the Father in no wise justifies an assumption of identity between Him and His Father.[5]

The LDS Prophet Brigham Young even made a similar claim that God was once a "finite being" and that God was at one time "fallen" as Adam was.[6] Additionally, in a very insightful glimpse into the mind of LDS Prophet Wilford Woodruff, we find this shocking admission:

> Some have said that I was presumptuous to say that Brother Brigham was my God and Savior, Brother Joseph was his God and the one that gave Joseph the keys of the kingdom was his God which was Peter. Jesus Christ was his God and the Father of Jesus Christ was Adam.[7]

LDS Apostle Heber Kimball also believed that one day he too would become a Savior for many.[8]

THE BIBLICAL VIEW

There is one eternal God (monotheism). He has revealed Himself in three persons within the Godhead: Father, Son, and Holy Spirit. He has revealed Himself as a self-contained Creator in essence and being.

If there are many gods, and the God of Scripture is actually a combination of entities, then how do we know which god is supreme? Is the Father supreme over Christ? Is Christ supreme over the Holy Spirit? If the Father is an exalted man and there was a god before Him, doesn't that tell us that the God we worship is not really the Creator of all things that exist? Who is the best god? Who is the god of all gods? According to LDS scriptures, God is only one in a series of gods spanning an eternity past.

Keep in mind here that the Mormons cite many LDS sources alongside biblical references. The reason is that the Mormon scriptures are at many points contradictory of each other. Great pains have been taken by Mormon apologists to explain these opposing statements. Many people have left the Mormon Church after realizing the degree of their indoctrination and the unreliability of official LDS teaching.

As an example of the Mormon confusion, consider that a statement by Joseph Smith that was originally included in *Doctrine and Covenants* has been edited out of subsequent editions in order to safeguard the doctrine of multiple gods:

> There are two personages who constitute the great, matchless, governing and supreme power over all things—by whom all things were created and made, that are created and made, whether visible or invisible: whether in heaven, on earth, or in the earth, under the earth, or throughout the immensity of space—They are the Father and the Son: The Father becoming a personage of the spirit. . . . The Son . . . was ordained from before the foundation of the world to be a propitiation for the sins of all those who should believe on his name, and is called the Son because of the flesh . . . and he being the only begotten of the Father, full of grace and truth, and having overcome, received a fulness of the glory of the Father—possessing the same mind with the

> Father, which mind is the Holy Spirit, that bears record of the Father and the Son, and these three are one . . . and these three constitute the Godhead, and are one . . . the Father, Son, and Holy Spirit are one.[9]

Also posing difficulty for polytheism is 3 Nephi 11, from the *Book of Mormon*. Christ is recorded as saying, "I am in the Father." Remember that Mormon theology teaches a plurality of gods and that Christ is not unified with the Father except in purpose. Three Nephi 11:27, 36, is a clear indication that Mormon theology has significantly changed since the original writing of the *Book of Mormon*:

> And after this manner shall ye baptize in my name; for behold, verily I say unto you, that the Father, and the Son, and the Holy Ghost are one; and I am in the Father, and the Father in me, and the Father and I are one. . . . And thus will the Father bear record of me, and the Holy Ghost will bear record unto him of the Father and me; for the Father, and I, and the Holy Ghost are one.

Another troublesome passage is 2 Nephi 11:7. It has been used by Mormons to say that Christ is the God of the earth, and the Father is the God of Christ. Therefore, LDS apologists conclude, Christ can be called God and the Father can be called God, but they should not be confused or referred to as one God in essence. However, this passage says explicitly that if Christ is not God, there is no other God. Period. There is no exception given in this Mormon scripture:

> For if there be no Christ there be no God; and if there be no God we are not, for there could have been no creation. But there is a God, and he is Christ, and he cometh in the fulness of his own time.

As we have seen, some of the most direct and damaging texts for the Mormon doctrine of a plurality of gods are from the *Book of Mormon*. Especially detrimental is 2 Nephi 31:21. Here the ontological unity of God is being discussed. Note that this verse has nothing to do with being one in purpose, but speaks of the essence of God Himself.

> And now, behold, this is the doctrine of Christ, and the only and true doctrine of the Father, and of the Son, and of the Holy Ghost, which is one God, without end. Amen.

We turn now to Mosiah 15:2–5. The heading for chapter 15 reads, "How Christ is both the Father and the Son." Note that the passage does not speak of Christ's being one in purpose with the Father, but instead it speaks of the ontological unity of Christ and the Father:

> And because he dwelleth in flesh he shall be called the Son of God, and having subjected the flesh to the will of the Father, being the Father and the Son—The Father, because he was conceived by the power of God; and the Son, because of the flesh; thus becoming the Father and the Son—And they are one God, yea, the very Eternal Father of heaven and of earth. And thus the flesh becoming subject to the Spirit, or the Son to the Father, being one God.

Keep in mind that even in the heading for Mosiah 15, Jesus is said to be Father and Son. Jesus is the Son only and exclusively. He is God, but He is not the Father. Herein is the mystery of the Trinity as revealed in Scripture. Three in person and one in essence. There can be no distinction in their essence and no confusion of their persons. To try to become more specific either adds to the teachings of Scripture or takes away from the teachings of Scripture. We must be very careful not to preach beyond what the Bible allows.

In addition, a few of the most disputed texts when it comes to the Mormon doctrine of a plurality of gods and the essential equality of Christ with the Father proclaim in straightforward terms that Christ is the eternal Father. These texts should be read in conjunction with Isaiah 9:6:

> Teach them that redemption cometh through Christ the Lord, who is the very Eternal Father. Amen. (Mosiah 16:15)

> And as I spake concerning the convincing of the Jews, that Jesus is the very Christ, it must needs be that the Gentiles be convinced also that Jesus is the Christ, the Eternal God. (2 Nephi 26:12)

> For unto us a child is born, unto us a son is given: and the government shall be upon his shoulder: and his name shall be called Wonderful, Counsellor, The mighty God, The everlasting Father, The Prince of Peace. (Isa. 9:6)

Alma 11 is probably used more than any other text to demonstrate that Mormon theology has shifted from its roots. Read this one carefully. Not only does Amulek state that there are not a plurality of gods, he also admits quite boldly that Jesus the Christ, the Holy Spirit, and the Father are one. Once again, there are no exceptions given to this statement.

> Now Zeezrom said: Is there more than one God? And he answered, No. Now Zeezrom said unto him again: How knowest thou these things? And he said: An angel hath made them known unto me. Now Zeezrom saith again unto him: Is the Son of God the very Eternal Father? And Amulek said unto him: Yea, he is the very Eternal Father of heaven and of earth, and all things which in them are; he is the beginning and the end, the first and the last. Now this restoration shall come to all, both old and young, both bond and free, both male and female, both the wicked and the righteous; and even there shall not so much as a hair of their heads be lost; but every thing shall be restored to its perfect frame, as it is now, or in the body, and shall be brought and be arraigned before the bar of Christ the Son, and God the Father, and the Holy Spirit, which is one Eternal God, to be judged according to their works, whether they be good or whether they be evil. (Alma 11:28–31, 38–39, 44)

In the New Testament, the Apostle Paul himself clarifies how many gods there are. In context, he is dealing with touching and eating foods sacrificed to idols. Paul says that though there may be things called idols or gods, there is only one God:

> As concerning therefore the eating of those things that are offered in sacrifice unto idols, we know that an idol is nothing in the world, and that there is none other God but one. For though there be that are called gods, whether in heaven or in earth, (as there be gods many, and lords many,) But to us there is but one God. . . . (1 Cor. 8:4–6)

How did the first people introduced to the *Book of Mormon* understand the unity of God? The Three Witnesses, who were later excommunicated from the LDS community, attested to the oneness of God:

> And the honor be to the Father, and to the Son, and to the Holy Ghost, which is one God.[10]

> Hast thou not known? hast thou not heard, that the everlasting God, the LORD, the Creator of the ends of the earth, fainteth not, neither is weary? there is no searching of his understanding. (Isa. 40:28)

Several other passages from Isaiah make it clear that if there were a plurality of gods, God Himself would know about it. God is reassuring Israel that there is no other god that can harm them; nor, indeed, does God have any knowledge of any other god.

> Thus saith the LORD the King of Israel, and his redeemer the LORD of hosts; I am the first, and I am the last; and beside me there is no God. . . . Fear ye not, neither be afraid: have not I told thee from that time, and have declared it? ye are even my witnesses.

> Is there a God beside me? yea, there is no God; I know not any. (Isa. 44:6, 8)

> I am the Lord, and there is none else, there is no God beside me: I girded thee, though thou hast not known me: That they may know from the rising of the sun, and from the west, that there is none beside me. I am the Lord, and there is none else. . . . Look unto me, and be ye saved, all the ends of the earth: for I am God, and there is none else. (Isa. 45:5–6, 22)

> Remember the former things of old: for I am God, and there is none else; I am God, and there is none like me. (Isa. 46:9)

Not only is there only one God, but the Apostles John and Paul both identify Christ as the Creator of everything that exists. He is described as being God and being with God. This is compatible with the Christian understanding, but quite inconsistent with present-day Mormon theology.

> In the beginning was the Word, and the Word was with God, and the Word was God. The same was in the beginning with God. All things were made by him: and without him was not any thing made that was made. In him was life; and the life was the light of men. . . . And the Word was made flesh, and dwelt among us, (and we beheld his glory, the glory as of the only begotten of the father,) full of grace and truth. (John 1:1–4, 14)

> Who is the image of the invisible God, the firstborn of every creature: for by him were all things created, that are in heaven, and that are in earth, visible and invisible, whether they be thrones, or dominions, or principalities, or powers: all things were created by him, and for him: And he is before all things, and by him all things consist. (Col. 1:15–17)

The God who spoke about Himself in the Old Testament book of Isaiah is very clear in His affirmation of Himself. This God is the only God there is. He is the very Creator of all things that exist. Jesus Christ, the Messiah prophesied in the Old Testament and manifested in the New Testament, equated Himself with the one true God of the Old Testament. He is called the Creator of all things, whether visible or invisible; *all* things were created by Him and for Him. Outside of Him, nothing exists. Praise God who is God alone.

We should expect to have some difficulties in understanding some things about God that He has revealed in Scripture. The Mormon is told that there are mysteries surrounding God that man is not able to fathom. This is true. However, God has explicitly revealed that there is only one God. Christ is not just one in purpose with the Father; He is one in essence with the Father as well. God has not left anything open to dispute concerning His nature. He has made Himself very clear throughout the testimony of His Prophets and Apostles in the Bible.

God has revealed Himself in three different persons: Father, Son, and Holy Spirit. God has further explained that there is no more than one God. How do we resolve this? Believe that He is one, and we will do well.

Men have tried to explain away the difficulties found in the revelation of God about Himself. The Apostle Paul, in Romans 1, tells us that natural man suppresses the Truth because of his unrighteousness. Those who do not believe in God as He has revealed Himself in Scripture will constantly try to rationalize that which they are not able to understand.

How should the Christian respond? Many are arrogant. Many mock those who do not believe in Christ. Is this what we are called to do according to Scripture? No. We are to correct them with gentleness and respect (2 Tim. 4:2; 1 Peter 3:15). We should pray for the grace of God to come into their lives. We should pray to the Lord that He awaken their hearts in worship and praise to Christ the Savior.

WHAT IS THE NATURE OF GOD?

THE LDS VIEW

It is the Mormon view that God was once a man, made of flesh and bone, and has been exalted to His current state. Given the doctrine of eternal progression, the Mormon Church also teaches that God still has a body of flesh and bone. Some members of the LDS Church claim that when God was exalted to godhood, He no longer consisted of blood but just flesh and bone. The reasoning behind this specific claim is unclear, but it is clear that the doctrine of God's being an exalted man is a major deviation from what Scripture teaches.

Official Mormon teaching on this subject may be sparse, but it does appear in *Doctrine and Covenants:*

> The Father has a body of flesh and bones as tangible as man's; the Son also; but the Holy Ghost has not a body of flesh and bones, but is a personage of Spirit.[11]

Apostle Bruce McConkie elucidates:

> False creeds teach that God is a spirit essence that fills the immensity of space and is everywhere and nowhere in particular present. . . . God the Father is a glorified and perfected Man.[12]

In the same vein is a statement by the Mormon Prophet Joseph Smith:

> God himself was once as we are now, and is an exalted man, and sits enthroned in yonder heavens. . . . We have imagined and supposed that God was God from all eternity. I will refute that idea, and take away the veil, so that you may see. . . . This is good doctrine. . . . When I tell you of these things which were given me by inspiration of the Holy Spirit, you are bound to receive them as sweet, and rejoice more and more.[13]

We also find a statement of LDS Prophet Wilford Woodruff that states that God, while He was a man, received His temple endowments "thousands and millions of years" ago.[14] Surely the Mormon Church would not be quick to distance itself from past Prophets, inspired Mormon scriptures, and official spokesmen. However, in an attempt to appear as a Christian organization to the outside world, maybe it will.

THE BIBLICAL VIEW

God is eternal. There is only one God. He did not progress from being a man to becoming a god.

If the God we worship was actually a man at one time, then He is not perfect from all eternity. If, as the Mormons claim, we can become as God is, then there really is nothing special or significant about God. He becomes a guide who merely helps us along our celestial voyage to perfection and godhood. He wouldn't deserve to be worshipped as perfect, unchangeable, omniscient, eternal, sovereign, or omnipresent. He would be an impotent ethereal exalted man who stumbled into having spirit-children who would one day be as great as He. But this is not the God of the Christian—the God of the Bible.

The Church of Jesus Christ of Latter-day Saints would have people believe that the Truth rests solely in their Restored Church of Christ. They claim that many important doctrines were left out of the Bible by heretics in the early Christian Church. One of the restored doctrines is that man can become like God in an eternal progression. Under this claim, God Himself progressed from being a man to becoming what He is today. The Mormons were not the first to give this false doctrine to mankind, nor was this idea left out of the Bible. We see it taught first in Genesis 3:5:

> For God doth know that in the day ye eat thereof, then your eyes shall be opened, and ye shall be as gods, knowing good and evil.

Though this doctrine may be taught in the Bible, it was not taught by God. The verse is a quotation of the words of Satan. This is the first statement in Scripture that directly assaults God's perfect nature. Satan was the first to suggest that man can become like God; Satan was first in claiming that there are other gods that can compare with the one and only God. The Prince of Lies concocted this doctrine.

Isaiah 43:10–11 is a very explicit repudiation of the Mormon doctrine of a progression of God from manhood to godhood. It also makes it clear that there has not been a progression of gods throughout all eternity:

> Ye are my witnesses, saith the LORD, and my servant whom I have chosen: that ye may know and believe me, and understand that I am he: before me there was no God formed, neither shall there be after me. I, even I, am the LORD; and beside me there is no saviour.

This text shows that Christ could not be a lesser god or a deity subservient to the Father: there is no God but the God of Isaiah. Also, Christ is presented in the New Testament as the Savior and as Lord. Mormon theology has no response.

Even the *Book of Mormon* contradicts this false view. The teaching of the Prophet Joseph Smith that God is not God from all eternity (see p. 70) directly contradicts Moroni 8:18:

> For I know that God is not a partial God, neither a changeable being; but he is unchangeable from all eternity to all eternity.

If Joseph Smith was a true Prophet, could he teach two opposite and competing doctrines of God?

We come now to texts that declare explicitly that God has been God from all eternity. The common LDS response is that God was once a man like us and later became the God we know today. He will be God from that point through all eternity. This view is refuted by both the Bible and various LDS writings:

> . . . the Lord Omnipotent who reigneth, who was, and is from all eternity to all eternity. (Mosiah 3:5)

> By these things we know that there is a God in heaven, who is infinite and eternal, from everlasting to everlasting the same unchangeable God, the framer of heaven and earth, and all things which are in them. (*Doctrine and Covenants* 20:17)

> Now unto the King eternal, immortal, invisible, the only wise God, be honour and glory for ever and ever. Amen. (1 Tim. 1:17)

Here we have a related group of passages asserting that God is not a man, that He has never been a man, and that He has not progressed to becoming God from manhood:

> And Ammon began to speak unto him with boldness, and said unto him: Believest thou that there is a God? And he answered, and said unto him: I do not know what that meaneth. And then Ammon said: Believest thou that there is a Great Spirit? And he said, Yea. And Ammon said: This is God. And Ammon said unto him again: Believest thou that this Great Spirit, who is God, created all things which are in heaven and in the earth? (Alma 18:24–28)

God is not a man, that he should lie; neither the son of man, that he should repent: Hath he said, and shall he not do it? or hath he spoken, and shall he not make it good? (Num. 23:19)

And also the Strength of Israel will not lie nor repent: for he is not a man, that he should repent. (1 Sam. 15:29)

Am I a God at hand, saith the LORD, and not a God afar off? Can any hide himself in secret places that I shall not see him? saith the LORD. Do not I fill heaven and earth? saith the LORD. (Jer. 23:23–24)

. . . for I am God, and not man. . . . (Hos. 11:9)

For I am the LORD, I change not; therefore ye sons of Jacob are not consumed. (Mal. 3:6)

But the hour cometh, and now is, when the true worshippers shall worship the Father in spirit and in truth: for the Father seeketh such to worship him. God is a Spirit: and they that worship him must worship him in spirit and in truth. (John 4:23–24)

Howbeit the most High dwelleth not in temples made with hands; as saith the prophet, Heaven is my throne, and earth is my footstool; what house will ye build me? saith the Lord: or what is the place of my rest? (Acts 7:48–49)

The most astonishing downplaying of the Mormon doctrine of God's being an exalted man comes from an interview with the Mormon Prophet Gordon Hinckley:

> On whether his church still holds that God the Father was once a man, he sounded uncertain, "I don't know that we teach it. I don't know that we emphasize it. . . . I understand the philosophical background behind it, but I don't know a lot about it, and I don't think others know a lot about it."[15]

How is it possible for an inspired and divinely appointed Prophet not to be aware of teachings concerning the God whom he worships?

To progress, one must be able to change. God, on the other hand, cannot change. God is the same from all eternity to all eternity. Once again, there are not even the slightest indications in these passages that God ever progressed from manhood to godhood.

5

BAPTISM FOR THE DEAD AND THE ORIGIN OF SIN

Baptism for the Dead

THE LDS VIEW

Baptism for the dead is a ceremony carried out in the LDS Temple to ensure salvation of those who would have chosen to follow the LDS Gospel but did not have an opportunity to do so while they were alive. A related doctrine is that of the spirit prison, where good spirits can minister to the bad spirits. Because Jesus bridged the gap between paradise and torment, the unrighteous can gain salvation even after death.

Keep in mind that neither doctrine is found in the *Book of Mormon*. But if the *Book of Mormon* contains the fullness of the Gospel according to LDS teaching, then why were the ordinance of baptism for the dead and the concept of their spirit prison introduced later? Are we to assume that the *Book of Mormon* is not complete?

James Talmage points out that no distinction is made between baptism for the dead and baptism for the living:

> Compliance with the ordinance has been shown to be essential to salvation, and this condition applies to all mankind. Nowhere in scripture is a distinction made in this regard between the living and the dead.[1]

Talmage proceeds to justify baptism for the dead on the basis of two statements made in 1 Peter:

> It is plain, then, that the Gospel must be proclaimed in the spirit world; and, that such work is provided for the scriptures abundantly prove. Peter, describing the mission of the Redeemer, thus declares this truth: For this cause was the gospel preached also to them that are dead, that they might be judged according to men in the flesh, but live according to God in the Spirit (1 Peter 4:6). The inauguration of this work among the dead was effected by Christ in the interval between His death and resurrection. While His body lay in the tomb, His spirit ministered to the spirits of the departed: By which also he went and preached unto the spirits in prison; Which sometime were disobedient, when once the longsuffering of God waited in the days of Noah, while the ark was a preparing, wherein few, that is, eight souls were saved by water (1 Peter 3:19–20).[2]

But Talmage's argument in no way nullifies any further debate over the doctrine. While it may be true in the LDS mind that there is no distinction between baptism for the living and for the dead, there is a distinction as to who is able to be saved: the living can be saved, the dead cannot.

Baptism doesn't even enter into the discussion. The very foundation of the LDS doctrine of baptism for the dead cannot be substantiated because salvation is not possible once a person has died.

The Apostle Paul comments on the lostness of man. In Romans 1 he says that all men know the Godhead, the eternal power, and the attributes of God. Those things are revealed to them in God's creation itself. But they reject that truth because of their unrighteousness. They hate God. They reject Him. With this in mind Prophet Gordon Hinckley asks a provocative question:

> Millions of people have died without hearing the gospel and receiving the necessary ordinances. What will happen to them? . . . We have the opportunity to go to a temple in behalf of the dead. In the temple, we can perform all the ordinances necessary for the exaltation of those who have died.[3]

A number of related statements help clarify the Mormon doctrines of baptism for the dead and spirit prison:

> Baptism of the living for the dead is performed in temples of the Lord erected to his name and at his command in this dispensation.[4]

> For a baptismal font there is not upon the earth, that they, my saints, may be baptized for those who are dead.[5]

> The work done by Elijah was to open the door of salvation for the dead. From that event comes the

> knowledge of the principles by which the saving power of the Gospel may be applied to men who have died without receiving its benefits in this life.[6]

> But behold, these which thine eyes are upon shall perish in the floods; and behold, I will shut them up; a prison have I prepared for them. And That which I have chosen hath pled before my face. Wherefore, he suffereth for their sins; inasmuch as they will repent in the day that my Chosen shall return unto me, and until that day they shall be in torment.[7]

John Widtsoe goes so far as to disagree with the direct teaching of Jesus Christ Himself. Jesus, in Matthew 25:44–46, says that some will go into eternal punishment. Christ doesn't pull any punches. He says that some will be condemned. Widtsoe, however, is emphatic:

> In the Church of Jesus Christ of Latter-day Saints there is no hell. All will find a measure of salvation. . . . The gospel of Jesus Christ has no hell in the old proverbial sense.[8]

Talmage takes a similar position:

> Upon all who reject the word of God in this life will fall the penalties provided; but after the debt has been paid the prison doors shall be opened, and the spirits once confined in suffering, then chastened and clean, shall come forth to partake of the glory provided for their class.[9]

THE BIBLICAL VIEW

Baptism for the dead cannot change condemnation to salvation, for Hell is eternal. Those who do not in this life accept the teachings of Jesus Christ as outlined in the Bible will be judged and sent to an eternal punishment with no opportunity to escape or second chance for salvation.

Even when the Apostle Paul mentions "baptism for the dead," he is not speaking of Christian teaching. In 1 Corinthians 15:29 we see that the opponents of the Apostle believed in baptism for the dead, while rejecting the teaching of the resurrection. Paul's response to them is that if there is no resurrection, why baptize for the dead? If they won't be raised, why do a proxy-baptism for them? Paul does not advocate baptism for the dead; he uses that false teaching as an object lesson to show the inconsistency of his adversaries.

The problem with the Mormon Church's position is not so much in the act of baptism for the dead. The discussion must also cover the issue of salvation after death. The Bible teaches in many places that those who die as unbelievers are no longer able to come to salvation. They have had their opportunity to believe. They died hating and denying God.

The *Book of Mormon* does not contain any teaching about baptism for the dead. If, as the Mormons claim, baptism for the dead is essential for salvation, and if the *Book of Mormon* contains the fullness of the Gospel, how can this practice be divinely acceptable? How can baptism for the dead effect salvation?

In fact, the *Book of Mormon* in two places affirms what the book of Hebrews says regarding the possibility of salvation after death: Once a person dies, then comes judgment. The *Book of Mormon* does not allow for the LDS doctrine of baptism for the dead because it does not allow for salvation after death.

> For that same spirit which doth possess your bodies at the time that ye go out of this life, that same spirit will have power to possess your body in that eternal world. For behold, if ye have procrastinated the day of your repentance even until death, behold, ye have become subjected to the spirit of the devil, and he doth seal you his; therefore, the Spirit of the Lord hath withdrawn from you, and hath no place in you, and the devil hath all power over you; and this is the final state of the wicked.[10]

> And, in fine, Woe unto all those who die in their sins; for they shall return to God, and behold His face, and remain in their sins.[11]

> And it is appointed unto men once to die, but after this the judgment. (Heb. 9:27)

We should also be aware of the problems with Talmage's interpretation of 1 Peter. The first problem is that the LDS doctrine teaches that one must, at some point, minister to souls that are in prison. According to the LDS doctrine, this is the very place where Jesus went before His resurrection. The New American Standard Bible more accurately relays the intention of 1 Peter 4:6:

> For the gospel has for this purpose been preached even to those who are dead, that though they are

> judged in the flesh as men, they may live in the spirit according to the will of God.

The initial assumption made by LDS theologians is that Peter is speaking about preaching to people who are presently dead. It should be suggested that the verse may be merely a reference to Christ's speaking to Christians who were later martyred. Two biblically consistent possibilities remain: Those who are dead were preached to while alive, and those from the Old Testament who believed in Christ are now being ministered to as they await the appearance of their Lord and God. They believed in the Messiah, and now they are able to meet Him face to face.

The second problem stems from the usage of 1 Peter 3:19–20: "By which also he went and preached unto the spirits in prison; which sometime were disobedient, when once the longsuffering of God waited in the days of Noah, while the ark was a-preparing, wherein few, that is, eight souls were saved by water." Talmage, in *Articles of Faith,* describes Jesus as ministering to spirits of the deceased.

Matthew Henry replies to the apparent difficulty:

> Observe here, 1. The preacher; Christ Jesus, who interested himself in the affairs of the church and of the world, ever since he was first promised to Adam, Gen. iii. 15. He went, not by a local motion, but by special operation, as God is frequently said to move, Gen. xi. 5. Mic. i. 3. Hos. v. 15. He went and preached, by his Spirit striving with them, and inspiring and enabling Enoch and Noah to plead with them, and preach righteousness to them, as 2 Pet. ii. 5. 2. The hearers; because they were dead and disembodied when the

> apostle speaks of them, therefore he properly calls them spirits now in prison; not that they were in prison when Christ preached to them, as the vulgar Latin translation and the popish expositors pretend.[12]

There are also examples of Mormon scriptures that, on the subject of the nature and duration of the punishment for those who reject God, agree in principle with the Old and New Testaments and thus contradict other Mormon statements:

> And according to the power of justice, for justice cannot be denied, ye must go away into that lake of fire and brimstone, whose flames are unquenchable, and whose smoke ascendeth up forever and ever, which lake of fire and brimstone is endless torment.[13]

> And finally, all ye that will persist in your wickedness, I say unto you that these are they who shall be hewn down and cast into the fire except they speedily repent. And now I say unto you, all you that are desirous to follow the voice of the good shepherd, come ye out from the wicked, and be ye separate, and touch not their unclean things; and behold, their names shall be blotted out, that the names of the wicked shall not be numbered among the names of the righteous, that the word of God may be fulfilled, which saith: The names of the wicked shall not be mingled with the names of my people.[14]

Extremely damaging to the Mormon idea of a spirit prison in contrast to an eternal Hell is 2 Nephi 28:21–22.

Nephi, according to the *Book of Mormon,* recorded a warning for all to heed. He said that Satan tries to pacify man and lead him into a place from which there is no deliverance. How does Satan do that? One way that Satan tricks men is to tell them there is no Hell. Many of the Mormon Prophets would do well to read this passage again for their own benefit:

> And others will he [Satan] pacify, and lull them away into carnal security, that they will say: All is well in Zion; yea, Zion prospereth, all is well—and thus the devil cheateth their souls, and leadeth them away carefully down to hell. And behold, others he flattereth away, and telleth them there is no hell; and he saith unto them: I am no devil, for there is none—and thus he whispereth in their ears, until he grasps them with his awful chains, from whence there is no deliverance.

The LDS Church would have us believe that those who are in spirit prison are able to hear the Gospel and be saved even after death. Ecclesiastes contradicts this belief:

> Whatsoever thy hand findeth to do, do it with thy might; for there is no work, nor device, nor knowledge, nor wisdom, in the grave, whither thou goest. (Eccles. 9:10)

In like manner Jesus' words in Matthew 13 do not indicate that those who have died will have opportunity to accept the Gospel after they have passed on:

> The field is the world; the good seed are the children of the kingdom. But the tares are the children of the wicked one; The enemy that sowed them is the devil; the harvest is the end of the world; and the reapers are the angels. As therefore the tares are gathered and burned in the fire; so shall it be in the end of this world. The Son of man shall send forth his angels, and they shall gather out of his kingdom all things that offend, and them which do iniquity; And shall cast them into a furnace of fire: there shall be wailing and gnashing of teeth. (Matt. 13:38–42)

Next, in Matthew 23, Jesus asks a rhetorical question. How will those who are condemned to Hell escape it? Note that He presupposes that there is an eternal Hell in His discussion with the Pharisees:

> Ye serpents, ye generation of vipers, how can ye escape the damnation of hell? (Matt. 23:33)

Jesus says that some will go to the place that has been prepared for Satan and his angels, and that it is an eternal punishment. It does not end. There is no escape. Jesus clarifies His position a little bit more:

> Then shall he say also unto them on the left hand, Depart from me, ye cursed, into everlasting fire, prepared for the devil and his angels. . . . And these shall go away into everlasting punishment: but the righteous into life eternal. (Matt. 25:41, 46)

The Apostle Paul echoes the teaching of Jesus:

> Who shall be punished with everlasting destruction from the presence of the Lord, and from the glory of his power. (2 Thess. 1:9)

Finally, the Apostle John, in a vision, describes what is the second death. Note that this is not a second life, but a punishment that unbelievers will be subjected to:

> But the fearful, and unbelieving, and the abominable, and murderers, and whoremongers, and sorcerers, and idolaters, and all liars, shall have their part in the lake which burneth with fire and brimstone: which is the second death. (Rev. 21:8)

The issue at hand has been settled by biblical texts. The futility of any attempt at squirming out from under the authority of Scripture should be obvious. By going to a partially ambiguous verse, Mormon theologians try to establish preaching to the dead as normative for the whole of Christian experience. Christ did this, whatever it was, once. We are not commanded to. We are not told how to. There is no possibility of salvation after death. Scripture must take precedence over the wishes of LDS theology.

The Church of Jesus Christ of Latter-day Saints teaches the doctrines of baptism for the dead and spirit prison. Ecclesiastes 9:10 and Matthew 25 make it explicitly clear, however, that once a person dies, there is no second chance. According to Scripture, nothing can be done to change the course of an individual's direction, whether it be for salvation or for condemnation, after the person has died. According to Scripture, the unrighteous will not be punished for a short duration, but forever.

If the verses that we have examined are indeed the true Scripture of Jesus Christ, then we all have an opportunity to gain eternal life and peace with God. But if we do not accept the Gospel, an eternal Hell is waiting. On the other hand, if Mormon doctrine is true, then the worst that can happen is that we all may go to prison for a while. Scripture states, however:

> But I will forewarn you whom ye shall fear: Fear him, which after he hath killed hath power to cast into hell; yea, I say unto you, Fear him. (Luke 12:5)

This is not a temporal setback! It is a matter of eternal significance!

The Origin of Sin

What is sin? Is sin a moral condition? Is sin something inherent in all mankind? The Mormon Church holds that man is fundamentally good. The Christian view, on the other hand, is that sin is a condition that falls on all the descendants of Adam, who represented us in the Garden of Eden.

Are we all guilty of sin? Must we be old enough to distinguish right from wrong to be held accountable for Adam's sin? What is the difference between Adam before the Fall and all of mankind after the Fall?

THE LDS VIEW

In the Mormon view of sin, one must be aware of the law to violate the law. Furthermore, without the Fall, Adam and Eve would not have been able to have children.

In a lengthy statement that gives tremendous insight into the Mormon doctrine of sin and the origin of sin, Bruce McConkie quotes quite a few LDS scriptures to demonstrate that Adam and Eve must have had the knowledge of good and evil before they sinned. Otherwise, says McConkie, they would have remained in a catatonic, emotionless, innocent state. He goes on to add that there can be no sin when no law has been established.

> A man sins when he violates his conscience, going contrary to light and knowledge—not the light and knowledge that has come to his neighbor, but that which has come to himself. He sins when he does the opposite of what he knows to be right. Up to that point he only blunders. One may suffer painful consequences for only blundering, but he cannot commit sin unless he knows better than to do the thing in which the sin consists. One must have a conscience before he can violate it. . . . Where there is no law given there is no punishment; and where there is no punishment there is no condemnation. (2 Ne. 9:25). He that knoweth not good from evil is blameless. (Alma 29:5). Sin cannot be committed unless laws are ordained (Alma 42:17) and unless people have knowledge of those laws so that they can violate them. Adam and Eve could not commit sin while in the Garden of Eden, although laws of conduct had already been established, because the knowledge of good and evil had not yet been given them. Unless they had partaken of the fruit of the tree of the knowledge of good and evil they would have remained in a state of innocence, having no

> joy, for they knew no misery; doing no good, for they knew no sin. (2 Ne. 2:23).[15]

A few additional passages in the LDS scripture teach that Adam and Eve would not have had children, eternal life, happiness, or any goodness unless they had sinned:

> And Eve, his wife, heard all these things and was glad, saying: Were it not for our transgression we never should have had seed, and never should have known good and evil, and the joy of our redemption, and the eternal life which God giveth unto all the obedient.[16]

> And now, behold if Adam had not transgressed he would not have fallen, but he would have remained in the garden of Eden. And all things which were created must have remained in the same state in which they were after they were created; and they must have remained forever, and had no end. And they would have had no children; wherefore they would have remained in a state of innocence, having no joy, for they knew no misery; doing no good, for they knew no sin.[17]

It is evident that LDS teaching claims that joy is dependent on misery's existence. But what will our life then be like in the eternal state? God has promised in His Word that there will no longer be suffering or pain. Will we then have no joy in Him? Will we not, rather, rejoice to be free from sin? The LDS passages cited lack consistency in applying the promises of God universally. Adam did have joy in the

Garden. He enjoyed every day with the presence of the Lord God Almighty. Clearly, the LDS community has not justified their position. Saying something is so does not make it so.[18]

THE BIBLICAL VIEW

All have sinned and are guilty of sin whether they are aware of the law or not.

As Paul explains very clearly in Romans 5:12, all men have sinned in Adam:

> By one man sin entered into the world, and death by sin; and so death passed upon all men, for that all have sinned.

How all men sinned in Adam is another discussion altogether. The main point is that in Adam, all men are guilty of the same sin. We are seen as lawbreakers and sinners. Only through God's grace are any of us saved. Saved from what? From the just punishment due to our sin. Mormons, by contrast, define salvation as exaltation to godhood. But if the Old and New Testaments are to be believed at face value, there is a much worse fate awaiting those who deny their responsibility to obey God's law. There is a severe punishment for sinning against God. We have the high calling to worship God as God and not as an exalted man. There can be no equality with the God of all that exists. He alone is God.

Not only have all sinned, but all are in bondage to that sin:

> For all have sinned, and come short of the glory of God. (Rom. 3:23)

> Knowing this, that our old man is crucified with him, that the body of sin might be destroyed; that henceforth we should not serve sin. (Rom. 6:6)

Strangely, the Mormon book of Moses states quite plainly that Christ died for the original sin of Adam and Eve; because of His atonement, no one for whom He died will be punished for that sin:

> Hence came the saying abroad among the people, that the Son of God hath atoned for original guilt, wherein the sins of the parents cannot be answered upon the heads of the children, for they are whole from the foundation of the world. And the Lord spake unto Adam, saying: Inasmuch as thy children are conceived in sin, even so when they begin to grow up, sin conceiveth in their hearts, and they taste the bitter, that they may know to prize the good.[19]

King David, however, gives us a straightforward contrary teaching on innocence and guilt. He claims that from birth the wicked go astray:

> The wicked are estranged from the womb: they go astray as soon as they be born, speaking lies. (Ps. 58:3)

This assumes that at birth there is something to be distinguished as wicked. This does not speak well for the Mormon doctrine that no such thing as original sin exists.

In addition, Scripture makes it clear that people are guilty of sin whether they know they are sinning or not. It is possible to sin without being aware of the law:

> And so thou shalt do the seventh day of the month for every one that erreth, and for him that is simple: so shall ye reconcile the house. (Ezek. 45:20)

> Which none of the princes of this world knew: for had they known it, they would not have crucified the Lord of glory. (1 Cor. 2:8)

It was also Christ's understanding that people are capable of sinning without being consciously aware of their sin. Otherwise, He would not have prayed the way He did:

> Father, forgive them; for they know not what they do. (Luke 23:34)

The Apostle John, too, briefly defeats the charge that transgression of the law is not sin in the case of someone ignorant of the law:

> Whosoever committeth sin transgresseth also the law: for sin is the transgression of the law. (1 John 3:4)

Various other passages from the New Testament can be adduced to demonstrate that man is by nature sinful. Man is guilty of Adam's sin (Rom. 5), and his nature is sinful from birth. Paul in Ephesians declares that we are so dead in sin that we can be made alive by God's grace alone:

> But God, who is rich in mercy, for his great love wherewith he loved us, Even when we were dead in sins, hath quickened us together with Christ, (by grace ye are saved;) . . . For by grace are ye saved

> through faith; and that not of yourselves: it is the gift of God: Not of works, lest any man should boast. (Eph. 2:4–5, 8–9)

> Having the understanding darkened, being alienated from the life of God through the ignorance that is in them, because of the blindness of their heart. (Eph. 4:18)

God had given Adam and Eve a command to obey. They did not follow His Word, thereby sinning. So, then, sin came from Adam's disobedience, not out of God's will to implement and fulfill a plan of salvation. There would have been no need for a plan of salvation if Adam had remained in a state of innocence. So much for the Mormon doctrine that man is fundamentally good.

A second problem with the LDS scriptures is found in Moses 5:11. Eve supposedly says that if it were not for sin, she would not have had children. However, Genesis 1:28 gives the command to have children:

> And God blessed them, and God said unto them, Be fruitful, and multiply, and replenish the earth, and subdue it: and have dominion over the fish of the sea, and over the fowl of the air, and over every living thing that moveth upon the earth.

This took place on the sixth day—before the Fall! Why, then, would God tell Adam and Eve to have children and also in the same creation week condemn having children, as claimed in Moses 5:11 and 2 Nephi 2:22–23? If having children depends on being sinful, there is a problem with what

is written in Genesis. God does speak about childbirth after the Fall, but He is telling the woman that He will increase her pain in childbirth and make it sorrowful (Gen. 3:16).

Similar in content to Genesis 1:28, Moses 2:27–28 states that during the time when God considered everything perfect and during the time before Adam and Eve sinned, He told them to be fruitful, multiply, and subdue the earth. Not only did God allow, even command, them to have children, He also established many good works for them to accomplish:

> And I, God, created man in mine own image, in the image of mine Only Begotten created I him; male and female created I them. And I, God, blessed them, and said unto them: Be fruitful, and multiply, and replenish the earth, and subdue it, and have dominion over the fish of the sea, and over the fowl of the air, and over every living thing that moveth upon the earth.

Remember the claim by Mormon leaders and scriptures that Adam and Eve before their sin were not able to do good works or have children? This text from the book of Moses does much damage to that claim.

A third problem is that Romans 3:23 does not say that most have sinned, but that all have sinned. Sin entered into this world by Adam (Rom. 5). All things were changed by his sin from that moment for all time. Mankind is subject to death. But if death is a condition of sin, how can an infant die if, as Mormons contend, infants are sin-free? The answer is that the infant is not sin-free. The argument from the LDS literature would have the reader believe that the idol worshipper does not sin until he realizes that he is wrong. LDS doctrine does not fit well with Scripture.

6

CREATION AND ADAM

Pre-Existing Spirit and Matter

THE LDS VIEW

Matter existed before the creation of the earth. Creation was an organization of matter into a tangible form. Our spirits were created in the pre-existence by God the Father and an eternal Mother.

This particular Mormon doctrine is used to promote other doctrines such as the progression of manhood to godhood and a plurality of gods. If the doctrine of pre-existence is incorrect, these other Mormon doctrines have no foundation in Truth.

> Pre-existence is the term commonly used to describe the pre-mortal existence of the spirit children of God the Father. Speaking of this prior existence in a spirit sphere, the First Presidency of the Church (Joseph F. Smith, John R. Winder, and Anthon H. Lund) said: All men and women are in the similitude of the universal Father and Mother, and are literally the sons

> and daughters of Deity; as spirits they were the offspring of celestial parentage. (*Man: His Origin and Destiny*, pp. 351, 355). These spirit beings, the offspring of exalted parents, were men and women, appearing in all respects as mortal persons do, excepting only that their spirit bodies were made of a more pure and refined substance than the elements from which mortal bodies are made. (Ether 3:16; *Doctrine and Covenants* 131:7–8). To understand the doctrine of pre-existence two great truths must be accepted: 1. That God is a personal Being in whose image man is created, an exalted, perfected, and glorified Man of Holiness (Moses 6:57), and not a spirit essence that fills the immensity of space; and 2. That matter or element is self-existent and eternal in nature, creation being merely the organization and reorganization of that substance which was not created or made, neither indeed can be (*Doctrine and Covenants* 93:29).[1]

Moses 3:5 emphasizes the doctrine of the pre-existence of matter:

> And every plant of the field [existed] before it was in the earth, and every herb of the field before it grew. For I, the Lord God, created all things, of which I have spoken, spiritually, before they were naturally upon the face of the earth. For I, the Lord God, had not caused it to rain upon the face of the earth. And I, the Lord God, had created all the children of men; and not yet a man to till the ground; for in heaven created I them; and there was not yet flesh upon the earth, neither in the water, neither in the air.

This text is in direct opposition to various passages in Scripture. Indeed, the chronology of the creation account given in Genesis is forgotten by the author of the book of Moses.

THE BIBLICAL VIEW

All things were created by the one eternal God at the time that the book of Genesis records as the creation week.

A number of verses in Scripture simply do not allow for a spiritual creation predating the creation of the physical. This demonstrates a great chasm between Mormon theology and biblical truth:

> Howbeit that was not first which is spiritual, but that which is natural; and afterward that which is spiritual. (1 Cor. 15:46)

> The burden of the word of the LORD for Israel, saith the LORD, which stretcheth forth the heavens, and layeth the foundation of the earth, and formeth the spirit of man within him. (Zech. 12:1)

> For by him all things were created, that are in heaven, and that are in earth, visible and invisible, whether they be thrones, or dominions, or principalities, or powers: all things were created by him, and for him: And he is before all things, and by him all things consist. (Col. 1:16–17)

The three texts we have cited describe in detail what took place during the creation of mankind. First, the form of flesh was made, and then a soul was created in that form. All things were made by God; there are no exceptions to what He is or to what He has made. Christ made all things. Read Genesis 1 and compare it to what the Apostle Paul says in Colossians 1:16–17. Christ is God. Christ is the Creator. There are no gods before God, there are no gods before Christ. He created all things during the period described in Genesis 1.

The Adam-God Doctrine

THE LDS VIEW

Adam is God. Adam is the Ancient of Days. Adam is Michael the Angel. Adam is the Natural and Spiritual Father of Jesus.

Strangely enough, the majority of Mormons do not accept this official doctrine. LDS authorities have commonly told members of the Mormon Church that non-Mormons falsely attribute the doctrine to Mormons in an attempt to undermine LDS teaching. In fact, I have spoken to LDS missionaries who have no idea that the Adam-God doctrine has been taught by Mormon Prophets. Others, who are aware of Brigham Young's statements on the subject, openly reject the doctrine and claim that non-Mormons simply misunderstood Young. Young made an unguarded statement, and Mormon-haters pounced on it as an obvious falsity, they say.

What is the history of the Adam-God doctrine? Brigham Young claimed that it was revealed to him by God Himself. If the doctrine is false, as many modern Mormons maintain, then Brigham Young gave false revelations about God. In his first public defense of the Adam-God doctrine, Young pointed out that many Latter-day Saints did not want to accept truth that had been revealed to him by God. Their unbelief prevented them from accepting that Adam is God:

> How much unbelief exists in the minds of the Latter-day Saints in regard to one particular doctrine which I revealed to them, and which God revealed to me—namely that Adam is our father and God. . . . Our Father Adam helped to make this earth, it was created expressly for him, and after it was made he and his companions came here. He brought one of his wives with him, and she was called Eve, because she was the first woman upon the earth. Our Father Adam is the man who stands at the gate and holds the keys of everlasting life and salvation for all his children who have or who ever will come upon the earth.[2]

Not only did Young claim that Adam is God, but he also claimed that Adam helped make the earth, and that the earth was created specifically for Adam. Also, Young states that Eve was so named because she was the first woman on the earth. Finally, he claims that Adam, who is the Father, holds the authority of salvation for all who live on the earth after him.

Some may say that the Adam-God doctrine was a creation of the mind of Brigham Young. Just a few lines after his reprimand of the rampant unbelief, however, Young defends the doctrine as coming not from him. He clearly states that he could not find anyone who was able to tell him this great truth until Joseph Smith did:

> But I could not find any man on the earth who could tell me this, although it is one of the simplest things

> in the world, until I met and talked with Joseph Smith.[3]

When we check carefully, we do find, not surprisingly, that Joseph Smith taught this same doctrine:

> Daniel in his seventh chapter speaks of the Ancient of Days; he means the oldest man, our Father Adam, Michael. . . . He [Adam] is the father of the human family and presides over the spirits of all men.[4]

Even the most casual look at Daniel 7:9–22 shows that Daniel was referring to God and not Adam or Michael.

So it does not appear that Brigham Young was teaching a novelty invented by himself. His predecessor, Joseph Smith, believed it and taught it as well. Nevertheless, Brigham Young did much to promote this teaching during his days as LDS Prophet.[5]

In an attempt to head off criticism of this revelation, Prophet Young posits possible objections and refutes them easily. For instance, he claims that Adam was not created on Earth, but existed beforehand on another planet similar to Earth. Then he and his associates brought this planet into existence:

> Well, says one, Why was Adam called Adam? He was the first man on the earth, and its framer and maker. He, with the help of his brethren, brought it into existence. Then he said, I want my children who are in the spirit world to come and live here. I once dwelt upon an earth something like this, in a

> mortal state, I was faithful, I received my crown and exaltation.[6]

We repeat: many Mormons are not aware of this teaching of Brigham Young and Joseph Smith. Those who are aware of this doctrinal assertion may be tempted to say that it was only one statement by Young and we should not quote him out of context. In response, the statements by Prophet Young made from 1854 to 1869 seem to be clear. Moreover, other documents indicate that the Adam-God doctrine is not just a one-time misstatement by or misquotation of Prophet Young:

> [Adam] is our Father and our God, and the only God with whom WE have to do. . . . Now, let all who may hear these doctrines, pause before they make light of them, or treat them with indifference, for they will prove their salvation or damnation.[7]

> He [Brigham Young] said that our God was Father Adam. He was the Father of the Savior Jesus Christ—Our God was no more or less than ADAM.[8]

> Brother Pratt also thought that Adam was made of the dust of the Earth, could not believe that Adam was our God or the Father of Jesus Christ—President Young said that he was, that he came from another world and made this. . . . He told broth. Pratt to lay aside his philosophical reasoning and get revelation from God . . . we should grow up in revelation so that principle would govern every act of

> our lives. He had never found any difficulties in leading this people since Joseph's death.[9]

> Prophet Young said Adam was Michael the Archangel & he was the Father of Jesus Christ & was our God & that Joseph taught [word illegible] this Principle.[10]

> Who begat him [Christ]? His Father, and his father is our God, and the Father of our spirits, and he is the framer of the body, the God and Father of our Lord Jesus Christ. Who is he? His is Father Adam; Michael; the Ancient of days. Has he a Father? He has! Had he a mother? He had. Now to say that the son of God was begotten by the Holy Ghost, is to say the Holy Ghost is God the Father, which is inconsistent, and contrary to all the revelations of God both Modern, and ancient.[11] [original text]

> Our spirits and the spirits of all the human family were begotten by Adam, and born of Eve.[12]

> B. Young says that Adam was the Father of Jesus Christ, both of his Spirit and Body, in his teachings from the stand.[13]

There are numerous other statements that verify that Brigham Young did teach the doctrine that Adam is the Father and is God Himself. At this point one who wishes to defend the Mormon Church may say that Brigham Young cannot speak for the other Prophets of the LDS Church and that, even if he did teach the Adam-God doctrine, he certainly stands alone with it. Yet other Mormon officials have in fact endorsed the Adam-God doctrine: George Q. Cannon, member of the First Presidency; Joseph Fielding Smith, who became the tenth Prophet of the LDS Church; and Lorenzo Snow, who became the fifth Prophet.[14] Another example is Heber Kimball, who was a Mormon Apostle in the mid 1800s:

> Brigham Young was certainly not the only early Mormon leader who had a testimony to the doctrine. Heber C. Kimball, a member of the First Presidency, claimed that, the Lord told me that Adam was my father and that he was the God and father of all the inhabitants of this earth. (*Dialogue: A Journal of Mormon Thought*, spring 1982, p. 27).[15]

There can be no doubt that Brigham Young and other Mormon leaders taught the Adam-God doctrine.

THE BIBLICAL VIEW

Adam was the first created man on the earth. God, being eternal and exclusively divine, is not to be equated with Adam. God is superior to and distinct from Adam.

A difficulty with this doctrine arose, as we have seen, within the Mormon Church. Keep in mind that although the majority of Mormons do not accept the Adam-God doctrine, it has nevertheless been taught by many Mormon Prophets. If this teaching proves to be false according to Scripture or is repudiated by other Mormon Prophets, those who teach or have taught the doctrine are false teachers.

We have determined that the Adam-God doctrine was taught by LDS officials. But was there any dissension from

this teaching throughout the LDS Church's history? There was. Has it been refuted by the Mormon Church? It has.

1. Apostle Orson Pratt denied Prophet Brigham Young's revelation as being contradictory to LDS scripture in April 1860. At a meeting of the Council of the Twelve, Pratt came under attack for his denial of Young's Adam-God doctrine. Of all the Mormon officials in attendance, only Pratt denied the doctrine. Pratt's words in the record of the meeting make his position clear:

> It was the Father of Jesus Christ that was talking to Adam in the garden—B. Young says that Adam was the Father of Jesus Christ, both of his Spirit and Body, in his teachings from the stand. Bro. Richards published in the Pearl of Great Price, that another person would come in the meridian of time, which was Jesus Christ. . . . I have heard brother Brigham say that Adam is the Father of our Spirits, and he came here with his resurrected body, to fall for his own children; and I said to him, it leads to an endless number of falls, which leads to sorrow and death: that is revolting to my feelings, even if it were not sustained by revelation . . . it was so contrary to every revelation given.[16]

Note that Pratt denies the teaching of Prophet Brigham Young. If, as Young prophesied, Adam was God, how is it possible that God spoke to Adam in the Garden? If Adam was God, wouldn't that mean he was talking to himself? Pratt is arguing that Scripture records two different beings speaking, not just one being entertaining himself.

Pratt continues his revolt against Young by saying that even if this prophecy were divine, it would still be appalling to him. Pratt cannot accept this doctrine as something that God revealed. The implication here is that if Pratt is right, Brigham Young gave false teachings, and the other Mormon Apostles involved in the meeting with Young and Pratt believed these false teachings. Pratt openly rejected the teachings of the Prophet who had established the LDS Church in Utah.

2. George Q. Cannon thought it unwise to teach the Adam-God doctrine to the people. As a member of the First Presidency at the turn of the twentieth century, Cannon believed the Adam-God doctrine. What is astounding is that he honestly felt that it should not be taught openly, and in November 1898 stated:

> The Prophet Brigham Young taught some things concerning that [the Adam-God doctrine]; but the First Presidency and the twelve DO NOT THINK IT WISE TO ADVOCATE THESE MATTERS.[17]

Why would a prophecy from God not be preached to the whole body of those who believe in Him? Also note that the reaction by the Council of the Twelve was not condemnation of Brigham Young's Adam-God doctrine. Instead, the response was to hide it from the public eye.

3. In direct opposition to Young's revelation, Apostle LeGrand Richards denied that the Adam-God doctrine is true. Having been questioned on the subject in May 1966, Richards responded with a letter that was unequivocal:

> Is the Adam God Doctrine, as taught in the *Journal of Discourses*, true? Answer: NO.[18]

4. The same month that LeGrand Richards wrote his letter of denial, Hugh Brown, of the First Presidency, also denied that Young's Adam-God doctrine was an official teaching of the LDS Church. In addition to denying that the Adam-God doctrine was true, Brown maintained that the account written in *Journal of Discourses* was not accurate. Here is evidence of the internal turmoil between different authorities within the LDS community:

> The Adam-god doctrine is not the doctrine of the church, and the reports on that subject as published in the *Journal of Discourses* are not accurate.[19]

About seventy years had passed from the counsel of George Q. Cannon until the time of Hugh Brown. During this period the official position of the LDS Church had gone from suppression of the teaching to outright denial.

5. Also in 1966 Prophet Joseph Fielding Smith contended that Prophet Young had not actually taught that Adam was the Father of Christ. Once again, the Mormon Church stands in a precarious place. To deny Prophet Joseph Fielding Smith is to deny a Prophet of God. To deny Brigham Young, and his alleged revelation, is to deny another Prophet of God.

Smith made a statement in direct opposition to the written testimonies of Wilford Woodruff, Orson Pratt, and others that Young had affirmed that Adam is the Father of Christ:

> In discussing the statement by President Brigham Young that the Father of Jesus Christ is the same

> character who was in the Garden of Eden, I maintain that President Young was not referring to Adam, but to God the Father, who created Adam, for he was in the Garden of Eden, and according to Mormon doctrine Adam was in his presence constantly, walked with him, talked with him, and the Father taught Adam his language.[20]

At this point in LDS history, we find equivocation of terms in defining exactly what Brigham Young had taught. Earlier statements were very clear in explaining the exact phrasing of Young's Adam-God doctrine. We should note that if Joseph Fielding Smith was correct, then all those who followed Brigham Young, and Young himself, simply misunderstood their own teachings. Although it may be desirable to redefine Young's position, this only leads to more suppression and covering up of embarrassing teachings within Mormon theology.

In October 1976, Spencer W. Kimball, the twelfth LDS Prophet, denounced the Adam-God doctrine of Joseph Smith and Brigham Young:

> We warn you against the dissemination of doctrines which are not according to the Scriptures and which are alleged to have been taught by some of the General Authorities of past generations. Such, for instance, is the Adam-God theory.
>
> We renounce that theory and hope that everyone will be cautioned against this and other kinds of false doctrine.[21]

6. Apostle Bruce R. McConkie, while admitting that Brigham Young did teach the doctrine that Adam is God, claims that anyone who believes that doctrine will be damned. That is to say, though Brigham Young taught the doctrine, he was wrong. McConkie refutes all those who deny that Brigham Young taught anything close to the Adam-God doctrine:

> Yes, President Young did teach that Adam was the father of our spirits, and all the related things that the cultists ascribe to him. This [doctrine], however, is not true. He expressed views which are out of harmony with the gospel.[22]

Here we have an unambiguous contradiction of Prophet Joseph Fielding Smith's statement on Young's Adam-God doctrine. McConkie flatly denies the truthfulness of Prophet Joseph Fielding Smith. So, at this point in LDS history, we have yet one more reversal on the teachings of Brigham Young and his associates.

McConkie also claims that Prophet Young's revelation is false and is contrary to God. He blatantly denies the validity of Brigham Young's teaching:

> In that same devotional speech I said: There are those who believe or say they believe that Adam is our father and our God, that he is the father of our spirits and our bodies, and that he is the one we worship. I, of course, indicated the utter absurdity of this doctrine and said it was totally false.[23]

Finally, McConkie gives a warning to all who believe the doctrines of Brigham Young:

> If we believe false doctrine, we will be condemned. If that belief is on basic and fundamental things, it will lead us astray and we will lose our souls. . . . This clearly means that people who teach false doctrine in the fundamental and basic things will lose their souls. . . . If we choose to believe and teach the false portions of his doctrines, we are making an election that will damn us.[24]

After reading McConkie's warning, one must conclude that if Brigham Young believed the Adam-God doctrine and claimed that it was revealed from God, he is damned to Hell because of his teaching. McConkie also taught that all who believe this false doctrine make an election that damns them. Was Prophet Young damned? One can only wonder.

Brigham Young's statement in *Journal of Discourses* stands in contrast to the denials and admonitions of McConkie:

> [Adam] is our Father and our God, and the only God with whom WE have to do. . . . Now, let all who may hear these doctrines, pause before they make light of them, or treat them with indifference, for they will prove their salvation or damnation.[25]

Whom should the LDS believe? If the Prophet Brigham Young was correct, is Bruce R. McConkie damned? Whose statements take precedence? At the very least, Young claimed that his teaching was a true revelation from God.

McConkie claimed that this teaching denied Scripture. Whom should the Mormon believe?

If Brigham Young was a true Prophet, then his words should stand as a warning to those Mormons who deny Young's Adam-God teaching. After all, he claimed that acceptance of this doctrine was a matter of eternal significance. Those who mock this revelation about Adam or think it is of no difference to their Mormon belief system are in tremendous salvific peril.

Here are the possibilities:

1. McConkie and the others who deny Young's teaching are wrong and have given false testimony against LDS Prophets. This would make Brigham Young's revelation true. Further, all who deny the teaching of Young would then be in danger of damnation for not accepting it.
2. Joseph Smith, Brigham Young, and some other Mormon Prophets have given false revelation and are false prophets. This would make McConkie and his party correct in their allegations.

It cannot be denied that the Adam-God doctrine was taught. Prophet Young claimed that he received it not only from God, but also from Joseph Smith. If this doctrine is denounced by the Mormon Church, then Joseph Smith stands indicted for the same crime as does Brigham Young. They gave false revelation and are false prophets.

The Mormon Church stands on the foundation of the doctrines of the authority of the Priesthood and the Restoration of the Church. They, in turn, stand on the validity of the LDS Prophets. If the Prophets were false and they misguided many people, how can their authority be valid? Can a false prophet pass along the authority of the Priesthood? This appears to present quite a problem for future LDS authorities to deal with.

One can only pray for the direction of the LDS Church. McConkie, in his many writings, demonstrated a desire to follow God. Yet he never could free himself from the demands and false teachings of the Mormon Church. We can, however, see in him and others like him a progressive shift away from anti-Christian doctrines. Encourage your Mormon friends to accept what Scripture has taught over that which man teaches.

7

THE *BOOK OF MORMON* AND THE BIBLE

An LDS gentleman once asked me, "Why is the LDS teaching so important to you?" That is a good question to keep in mind. The primary reason any such question should be asked is that we are commanded to study the whole counsel of God. If Joseph Smith or any other person claims to have received special revelation from God, we are to test every single piece of that revelation and compare it with Scripture. If the *Book of Mormon, Doctrine and Covenants,* and *Pearl of Great Price* are products of Smith's imagination, we might expect him to get most of the information correct and in accord with the Bible. But somewhere and at some point, if he is false, he will expose his falsity by his own words. There may be small errors or large doctrinal differences; we must look at those areas and evaluate them carefully.

James Talmage summarizes some of the foundations that are put forward for the authenticity of the *Book of Mormon:*

> The general agreement of the Book of Mormon with the Bible in all related matters. . . . The strict agreement and consistency of the Book of Mormon with itself.[1]

This claim is rather odd. To declare that the *Book of Mormon* and the Bible are generally in agreement while the *Book of Mormon* must be in strict agreement with itself is a low demand on the validity and truth of the *Book of Mormon* and the Bible. Why would any person who claims to believe in Christ as Savior not demand complete and strict agreement between texts that are said to be divinely inspired?

Further, as has been demonstrated throughout this study, the *Book of Mormon* is at many points not in agreement with the Bible or the other Standard Works of the Mormon Church. This falls short of the standard stressed by Bruce McConkie:

> The Lord's house is a house of order, and one truth never contradicts another. (*Doctrines of Salvation*, 3:203–4).[2]

The leaders of the Mormon Church have attempted to explain these differences away by theological sleight of hand and have been found lacking. Some who see the errors simply disregard them; others choose to accept the errors and continue to live an unhealthy inconsistency. Many people within the LDS Church who have attempted to make sense of some of the problem teachings have left the LDS Church permanently. While leaving the Mormon Church may mean being ostracized from one's family or community, it is a matter of eternal salvation. A person would be wiser

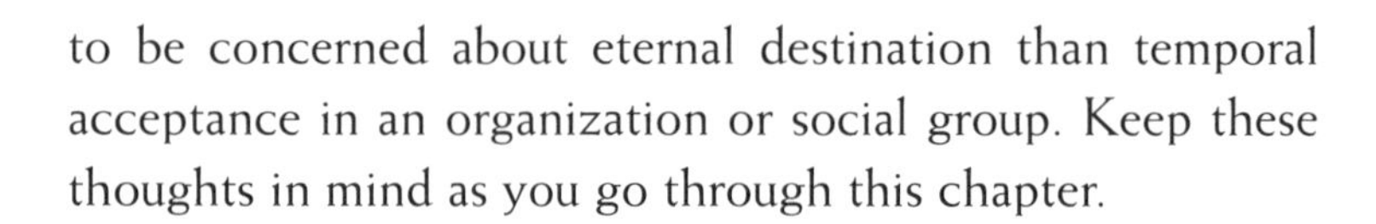

to be concerned about eternal destination than temporal acceptance in an organization or social group. Keep these thoughts in mind as you go through this chapter.

Did Joseph Smith Finish His Translation of the Bible?

The LDS view is that the King James Version is acceptable for use, but it is not a correct translation. A Great Apostasy in the Christian Church has corrupted the Bible. Consequently, alleges the Mormon Church, God commissioned a new translation.[3]

According to *Doctrine and Covenants* 73:3–4, the Bible was corrupted by the Christian Church after the Apostles died out. So God Himself issued a prophecy to Joseph Smith:

> Now, verily I say unto you my servants, Joseph Smith, Jun., and Sidney Rigdon, saith the Lord, it is expedient to translate again; And, inasmuch as it is practicable, to preach in the regions round about until conference; and after that it is expedient to continue the work of translation until it be finished.

Also keep in mind here the message of 1 Nephi 3:7. This text makes a very important point: God would have prepared a way for Joseph Smith to translate the Bible before he died. If not, Nephi is lying about the way God gives commandments:

> The Lord giveth no commandments unto the children of men, save he shall prepare a way for them

> that they may accomplish the thing which he commandeth them.

Now, Joseph Fielding Smith, the tenth Mormon Prophet, claimed that Joseph Smith did not finish translating his Restored Bible. And so Mormon leaders attempt to justify the prophecy that Joseph Smith would translate the Bible. They claim that he did not fail because his "intention" was to translate the Bible, but he was killed before the prophecy was able to be fulfilled.

> The reason that it [the Bible] has not been published by the Church is due to the fact that this revision was not completed. . . . It is recorded in the *History of the Church* that this was his intention. Due to persecution and mobbing this opportunity never came, so that the manuscript was left with only a partial revision.[4]

The difficulty with this view is that Joseph Smith did, according to his own account, finish all that was required to result in a Restored Bible:

> We this day finished the translating of the Scriptures, for which we returned gratitude to our Heavenly Father.[5]

Questions inevitably arise. Was the prophecy an "intention" of Joseph Smith, or was he really told by God that he would translate the Bible and complete the work? If this was indeed a revelation, and Joseph Smith did not complete the revision, he would be teaching false prophecies, which in turn would make him a false prophet.

Here are the possibilities:

1. The Mormon Prophet Joseph Smith lied. He did not receive the prophecy that is recorded in *Doctrine and Covenants* 73. First Nephi 3 says that God does not give any commandments unless He also supplies the means to fulfill them. Therefore, since God can't lie, Joseph Smith lied. This would make Joseph Smith a false prophet.
2. The Mormon Prophet Joseph Fielding Smith lied. If Joseph Smith did in fact finish translating the Bible according to prophecy, thus fulfilling 1 Nephi 3 and *Doctrine and Covenants* 73, Joseph Fielding Smith would be a false prophet.
3. Nephi lied. If the writer of the book of 1 Nephi did not actually believe that God would provide the means to fulfill commandments and falsified the account in his book, the writer of 1 Nephi would be a false prophet.
4. God lied. Giving inaccurate information, whether to Joseph Smith about his ability to complete a translation of the Bible, or to the writer of 1 Nephi about the fulfillment of commandments, or to Joseph Fielding Smith about Joseph Smith's work, would make God a lying God, and we wouldn't be able to trust Him about anything.

Any way one looks at the possibilities, Mormon theology is caught in quite a sticky place.

WHAT ABOUT THE BOOKS NOT IN THE BIBLE?

The Mormon Church claims completeness of the *Book of Mormon* while maintaining that the Bible is insufficient because current editions do not include certain books. Earlier in this study, however, we saw that the Mormon Prophets and some of the Standard Works of the LDS Church claim that the Bible does include the fullness of the Gospel. At the same time the Mormon Church still maintains that the *Book of Mormon* must be accepted as true and a person must belong to the LDS Church to hear the true Gospel.

James Talmage in *Articles of Faith*, an LDS document, lists a series of books not included in the present-day Bible: the Book of the Covenant; Book of the Wars of the Lord; Book of Jasher; Book of the Statutes; Book of Enoch; Book of the Acts of Solomon; Book of Nathan the Prophet, and that of Gad the Seer; Book of Ahijah the Shilonite, and the Visions of Iddo the Seer; Book of Shemaiah; Story of the Prophet Iddo; Book of Jehu; the Acts of Uzziah, by Isaiah, the son of Amoz; Sayings of the Seers; a missing Epistle of Paul to the Corinthians; a missing Epistle to the Ephesians; a missing Epistle to the Colossians, written from Laodicea; a missing Epistle of Jude; a declaration of belief mentioned by Luke. Talmage goes on to state the reason the Bible is not complete:

> Those who oppose the doctrine of continual revelation between God and His Church, on the ground that the Bible is complete as a collection of sacred scriptures, and that alleged revelation not found therein must therefore be spurious, may profitably

> take note of the many books not included in the Bible, yet mentioned therein, generally in such a way as to leave no doubt that they were once regarded as authentic.[6]

In an attempt to justify adding LDS scriptures to the canon, various Mormon texts charge that the Bible is not complete:

> For behold, they have taken away from the gospel of the lamb many parts which are plain and most precious; and also many covenants of the Lord have they taken away.[7]

> And gave him power from on high, by the means which were before prepared, to translate the Book of Mormon; Which contains a record of a fallen people, and the fulness of the gospel of Jesus Christ to the Gentiles and to the Jews also.[8]

> Behold, this is wisdom in me; wherefore, marvel not, for the hour cometh that I will drink of the fruit of the vine with you on the earth, and with Moroni, whom I have sent unto you to reveal the Book of Mormon, containing the fulness of my everlasting gospel, to whom I have committed the keys of the record of the stick of Ephraim.[9]

> And I have sent forth the fulness of my gospel by the hand of my servant Joseph; and in weakness have I blessed him.[10]

> And again, the elders, priests and teachers of this church shall teach the principles of my gospel, which are in the Bible and the Book of Mormon, in the which is the fulness of the gospel.[11]

The Bible, however, proclaims that it is sufficient for all the truth that God deems necessary for man to learn about the Gospel. The *Book of Mormon* is not scriptural, nor is it true.

The argument used by the LDS Church to justify an additional testament to Jesus Christ is based on the assumption that the books in its list of missing works are scriptural and necessary to complete the Bible. At the same time, the LDS Church claims that the *Book of Mormon* is complete, yet neither the *Book of Mormon* nor *Doctrine and Covenants* nor *Pearl of Great Price* contains those books either. By the same logic, the Standard Works of the Mormon Church must be incomplete.[12]

That the canon of Scripture that we are currently using does not contain the books mentioned by Talmage does not mean that the Bible is incomplete. The Apostle Paul, in Acts 17:28, quotes Greek poets. Does this mean that all the works of those poets should also be included in the Bible? Is the Bible incomplete because they aren't included?

Further, the Apostle Paul claimed that the Holy Scriptures were sufficient to lead a person to salvation:

> But continue thou in the things which thou hast learned and hast been assured of, knowing of whom thou hast learned them, and that from a child thou hast known the holy scriptures, which are able to make thee wise unto salvation through faith which is

> in Christ Jesus. All scripture is given by inspiration of God, and is profitable for doctrine, for reproof, for correction, for instruction in righteousness. (2 Tim. 3:14–16)

What did the first-century Christians regard as coming from God? The Old Testament. They couldn't possibly know of the writings of ancient Meso-Americans thousands of miles away on an entirely different continent.

We come back to the central question: What exactly is the Gospel and what exactly is faith? This is the heart of the matter before us. Whoever claims that the *Book of Mormon* contains the fullness of the Gospel and that the Church of Jesus Christ of Latter-day Saints is the only true Church must carefully define what is meant. What is a true Church? What must it teach? Was no true Gospel taught from the time of the Apostles to the time of Joseph Smith? What must one believe or do to be saved? What is salvation? The answers to these questions are central to understanding the differences between the Mormon Church and the church that you attend.

8

THE ETHICAL ARGUMENT AGAINST MORMONISM

In this chapter we will look at more foundational issues of disagreement between orthodox Christianity and LDS doctrines. Although this entire work is devoted to demonstrating the many inconsistencies in and dangers associated with Mormon theology and philosophy, we will now take a brief look at the ethics of the Latter-day Saints. The impossibility of the LDS position will be demonstrated by the ethical and moral argument in the pages that follow.

The preceding chapters have pointed out the departure of the Latter-day Saints from the truths of Scripture. We have here more than a simple disagreement on minor doctrines. The LDS Church maintains that it is the sole authority able to dispense the essential truths of the Bible. Its authorities claim that the Mormon organization has brought the Gospel, lost for almost eighteen hundred years, back to the world. And yet the LDS community is not in agreement with the Bible on the character and nature of

God. Accordingly, we must look at the extent of their departure from the other teachings of Scripture as well.

Many in non-LDS circles have heard the statement, "Well, they might be a cult, but at least they are ethical and moral in politics and religious persuasion." There are many variations of this theme, but the idea is still the same: At least they're moral.

In this chapter, we will look at the claim that the LDS Church and its teachings are basically moral. There is no doubt that many will, on the basis of the statements already made, be hasty to accuse the author of saying that LDS members are immoral. That is not the accusation. The position presented in this chapter is this: The LDS Church and the teachings of the LDS Prophets are not based on the Christ of the Scriptures and therefore are not based on Christ, making the teachings of the LDS Church biblically *amoral* at best.

Furthermore, Mormons can give no logical foundation for their way of life. Their philosophy of thought is baseless because of their faulty doctrine of God. They can give no logical, rational, or biblical response to their critics because of that doctrinal unintelligibility. The God revealed in Scripture, it must be remembered, is the very foundation of all thought. Without Him, nothing is possible.

Absolute Morality

In chapter 4 we examined the LDS belief that God was once a man. This doctrine has a profound effect upon the foundations of morality. If God were once a man, He would not be eternally absolute. If God the Father were once a man, it would be impossible for Him to be the only Creator in the history of the universe. If He were a man at one time, He would at some point have had to rely on yet another creator in order to exist. In LDS theology, God is one among a progression of gods. If this is true, He is not eternal in being, knowledge, power, or deity. On the other hand, Scripture claims in many places that God has never changed, does not change, and will never change in the future. He is eternal in all aspects. He is the same "King eternal, immortal, invisible, the only wise God" (1 Tim. 1:17).

The god of LDS theology, of necessity, is progressing in strength and wisdom. He is growing in power. He is spreading his influence throughout the universe as time goes on. More of his spirit-children are taking more worlds into their dominion. The god of LDS doctrine was once a man, is limited in all matters, is progressing in all things, and eventually achieved godhood. Man receives glorification in the LDS doctrines of salvation. Salvation in this worldview is nothing but sinful people achieving godhood.

The God of the Bible, by contrast, possesses all knowledge (Matt. 6:8; 1 Cor. 2:7; Heb. 4:13; 1 John 3:20). He is all-powerful (Job 5:9–27; 26:14; Ps. 62:11; 115:3; Isa. 40:26; Eph. 1:11). He has dominion over all of creation (Dan. 4:25, 35; 1 Tim. 6:15; Rev. 4:11). His Gospel is being preached to all people everywhere (Matt. 28:18–20; Rom. 10:14–15; Phil. 1:18). The God of the Bible is perfect, glorious, majestic, and eternal (Job 11:7–9; Acts 7:2; 1 Tim. 1:17). The Bible gives all glory to God alone (Rom. 11:36; Eph. 1:6, 12, 14).

If God changed in the past, He is progressive and necessarily not eternal or absolute in any aspect. But if God is eternally the same, He is able to impose absolute commands and requirements on His creation. If not, He is able to give only suggestions, not moral imperatives. The Bible has much to say about the topic of the immutability of God. Malachi 3:6 states that God does not change. There is no question with the author of this book about God's nature. James 1:17 states: "Every good gift and every perfect gift is from above, and cometh down from the Father of lights, with whom is no variableness, neither shadow of turning." If God changed, wouldn't the authors of the Bible be the first to know?

God's moral laws are not eternally binding if He is growing in knowledge. If God came to a time when He was more complete than He was in the past, He is not perfect in learning. What is the level to which He must come in order to say of Him, "He knows all things"? Does the god of LDS theology know all those things that the god who created him knows? Does that god know the prehistory of his existence?

If there is even one thing that God does not know, He cannot be said to be omniscient. If the god of the *Book of Mormon* is still progressing to some degree or another, there may be morality issues that he has not resolved or even learned. The gods before him and after him may know better than he does.

Psalm 147:5 declares, "Great is our Lord, and of great power: his understanding is infinite." Notice that the psalmist is not speaking of a god that is limited in any sense. The God of Scripture is absolute in His knowledge and wisdom and understanding.

So we see that God's moral laws are not universal and unchanging in LDS theology. The Bible, however, presents God as one who does not change. His laws are never changing, His statutes fixed and unerring, as Paul proclaims: "For of him, and through him, and to him, are all things: to whom be glory for ever. Amen" (Rom. 11:36).

Moral rules and laws necessarily require an absolute and unchanging source to establish their nature as universal and binding. Hebrews declares that we have such a God: "Wherein God, willing more abundantly to shew unto the heirs of promise the immutability of his counsel, confirmed it by an oath" (Heb. 6:17). God does not change His counsel. He will never change His ethical standards. He has made this promise to mankind.

THE SINFULNESS OF NON-CHRISTIAN MORALITY

In the previous chapters of this book we looked at the LDS teaching on God. We concluded that the official LDS doctrines concerning God are not in accord with the Old and New Testaments in matters of ontology and eternality. There are other areas where we will find disagreements between Scripture and LDS teachings, but at the foundation the LDS Church starts with a false view of God.

With a false view of who God is, the LDS community cannot use the God of Scripture as the basis of any philosophy of biblical ethics. Therefore, the LDS cannot claim sole dependence on God as the author of their ethics. The ethical position of the LDS Church may appear on the surface to be identical to biblical ethics. However, if one does not base one's position on the God who is found in the Bible, then one's ethics are not biblical and are therefore opposed to biblical ethics. In short, nonbiblical ethics are essentially sinful.

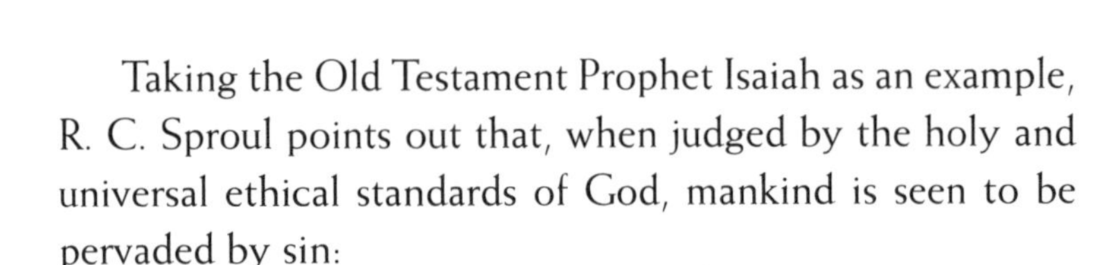

Taking the Old Testament Prophet Isaiah as an example, R. C. Sproul points out that, when judged by the holy and universal ethical standards of God, mankind is seen to be pervaded by sin:

> But if God is and if He is the Lord of the human race, the Creator of all of us, and if He holds us accountable to Him, then there is an objective standard of what is right in His sight. . . . We consider Isaiah in the temple when he had a vision of the holiness of God. He disintegrated before that appearance of God's majesty and cried out, "Woe is me, for I am undone, for I am a man of unclean lips." And then he went on to say, "And I dwell in the midst of a people of unclean lips." Isaiah recognized that his sinfulness was not unique. The fact that he recognized that other people were also guilty of the same sins did not mean that he was entertaining a judgmental spirit toward those other people. He was simply recognizing the truth of the matter: God was sovereign and holy in relation not only to him but to everybody else as well.[1]

Isaiah illustrates the human response to the holiness of God. The reaction is both terror and elation when man is confronted with the Holy. Isaiah was compelled to recognize that God is sovereign over all authorities in Heaven and Earth, and His authority sets the standard for our human condition. A Prophet like Isaiah would never imagine that he could achieve that which belonged only to the perfect and majestic God of the Bible! Isaiah does not paint a picture of achieving godhood; he gives an example of subjection to the absolute God.

God's ethics apply to all of mankind whether mankind recognizes that authority or not. His is an objective standard of righteousness. All those whose standard of personal ethics is not based on God's revealed will are not relying exclusively on God as their moral basis. Their ethics are not based on absolute standards but are anthropocentric in origin.

THEISTIC MORAL RELATIVISM

Some may argue that LDS ethical teachings are no different from the high moral standards of Scripture and are directly attributable to scriptural revelation. But a system whose god has changed his moral stance on even one point has a god who is not eternally consistent with his revealed statements. There are many striking examples of changes within LDS doctrine regarding God and His ethical teaching. However, we will cover only the Mormon view of plural marriage to prove our case.

In 1843 the prophetic word allowing polygamy, a word that God would revoke in 1890 during the quest for Utah statehood, was revealed to Joseph Smith as morally binding on all LDS:

> In the early days of this dispensation, as part of the promised restitution of all things, the Lord revealed the principle of *plural marriage* to the Prophet. Later the Prophet and leading brethren were commanded to enter into the practice, which they did in all

> virtue and purity of heart despite the consequent animosity and prejudices of worldly people.[2]

Note the ethical justification: polygamy was pursued "in all virtue and purity of heart."

The original revelation to Joseph Smith is found in *Doctrine and Covenants* 132. God tells Prophet Smith that multiple wives are allowable within certain boundaries of moral and ethical restraints. God's character and His immutable laws were called on, first, to validate the practice of plural marriage in the Old Testament and then to ratify it for Smith's contemporaries as well.

At the beginning the prophecy states:

> For behold, I reveal unto you a new and everlasting covenant; and if ye abide not by that covenant, then are ye damned; for no one can reject this covenant and be permitted to enter into my glory. (*Doctrine and Covenants* 132:4)

Throughout the remainder of the prophecy, ethical and absolute laws are appealed to in order to justify what must have been a very shocking statement coming from Joseph Smith: God was directly endorsing polygamy as a practice to be observed in the LDS community.

Also worth noting here is a statement of Joseph F. Smith:

> The eternal union of husband and wife and of plural marriage, is one of the most important doctrines ever revealed to man in any age of the world. . . . Without it we never could be exalted to associate

> with and become gods, neither could we attain to the power of eternal increase.[3]

In 1890, the doctrine was repealed by the ruling authorities of the LDS Church:

> At that time conditions were such that the Lord by revelation withdrew the command to continue the practice, and President Wilford Woodruff issued the Manifesto directing that it cease.[4]

Bear in mind that the original prophecy given to Joseph Smith was supposed to be an eternal command issued by God Himself. Then, forty-seven years later, it was revoked.

What we have seen is that God supposedly changed from prohibiting to allowing plural marriage in the 1840s and then changed back again in the 1890s. This is surely not a God who can never change His ethical standards.

If God is to be found true in every circumstance, and if morality is to be applicable in a uniform, consistent, and absolute way, then we must have a universal standard for ethical judgments. What the LDS Church has been promoting, however, have been nothing more than moral suggestions, not universal laws or standards of ethics. If the ethics of God can change, we have no basis for founding any moral law in Him. If God does not proceed by absolute standards, how can we?

Social Action

The LDS Church is committed to evangelization and social action. But if our conclusions thus far are true, LDS

preaching, mission work, and political involvement are directly opposed to Christ and His Word.

In Matthew 28:19 Christ commands, "Go ye therefore, and teach all nations, baptizing them in the name of the Father, and of the Son, and of the Holy Ghost." If, however, the philosophy and theology of the LDS Church are, at their very foundation, not based on Christ, then the work of LDS missionaries and the public presentation of Latter-day Saint messages about the *Book of Mormon* are false. The words of Christ and of His Apostles leave no room for equivocation. Paul said very plainly in Galatians 1:8–11:

> But though we, or an angel from heaven, preach any other gospel unto you than that which we have preached unto you, let him be accursed. As we said before, so say I now again, If any man preach any other gospel unto you than that ye have received, let him be accursed. For do I now persuade men, or God? or do I seek to please men? for if I yet pleased men, I should not be the servant of Christ. But I certify you, brethren, that the gospel which was preached of me is not after man.

Being the servant of Christ is the center of Paul's understanding of the Gospel. Becoming a god is not part of the Gospel. One cannot present the absolute truthfulness of God and His Word and at the same time preach the primacy of man. God does not permit this kind of idolatry.

What has become ever more apparent as this study has progressed is that LDS theology is very centered on man in direct opposition to being centered on God. The whole of the Christian life, however, is to be based on the glory of

God, not on the glory of the creature or creation. The Apostle Paul, in Ephesians 1:6, states that the purpose of our salvation is "the praise of the glory of his grace, wherein he hath made us accepted in the beloved." In verse 11 Paul goes on to say that God works all things according to the counsel of His own will, and in verse 12 that this is so in order that all things "should be to the praise of his glory." And finally in verse 14 Paul says that our redemption is "unto the praise of his glory." Note that nothing having to do with our salvation is done solely and exclusively for our specific benefit. Salvation does benefit mankind, but everything done on our behalf is for God's glory. There is a definite difference between the messages of Scripture and those of the LDS Prophets and writings.

Once again, if there are no absolute standards of ethics in LDS theology that have been given by God Himself through His Word, then LDS missionaries have no way to justify any statement of truth or morality. They have no claim on the Christ of Scripture. They are changing the very focus of Scripture, which is that God is the foundation of all thought and philosophy. Without Him all else is unintelligible.

The Inadequacy of the Mormon Position

The LDS cannot justify belief in their material. With no absolute standard by which to judge, the LDS community cannot critique opposing arguments. There is no logical refutation that they can present in order to challenge any biblical argument offered up against them. That which does not rely exclusively on the unchanging Truth of God is philosophically bankrupt.

Any attempt to argue against a universal standard is by definition not binding. If one were to argue, "Truth is relative," that argument itself is an absolute statement of Truth. To rely on absolutes in order to argue against them is self-defeating and self-deceiving.

Further, if a missionary from the Latter-day Saints wishes to convince us of the truthfulness of the *Book of Mormon,* he must do so on the basis that all "truth" in the *Book of Mormon* is founded in God's perfect character. But we have seen that the truthfulness of the *Book of Mormon* rests on a fallible god, so that Truth is subject to change. The promise to save could in fact condemn.

If, as in the Mormon system, there were no uniform nature in the way God deals with mankind, we would have no reason to believe His words. If there were no uniformity in Truth, there would be no coherence between facts, and no way to connect one proposition to another. Facts themselves would have no correspondence to one another. All rational interaction between subjects would be forfeited. In this case, Mormon missionaries would have no way to relate any topic to us or to make sense out of it.

If God is truly the Creator, on the other hand, all Truth is unified in Him and all things are maintained by Him. If absolute principles, ideals, laws, universal standards, and ethical judgments do in fact exist, then they must be derived from the absolute and unchanging God. If God is not our standard, then by what standard shall we judge matters of Truth? If God is not the authority, we are setting *ourselves* up as that authority.

The whole of the argument presented here is not about placing verses of the Bible against each other in an effort to disprove LDS doctrines. The discussion is not about individual facts, but the nature of facts and our interpretation of them. Furthermore, if we believe that the whole of Truth that God has delivered is unified and based solely in Himself, we expect that no two passages of Scripture can be pitted against each other.

Now, if God were subject to change or progression, the Bible would be in error. If God were in error or the Bible in error, we would have no basis from which to know any truth. But God is the basis of all rational endeavors. Even those who deny Him are forced to borrow His truths in order to argue against Him. Not only is this process self-deceptive, it is a demonstration of the inescapability of God's Truth in this world. Romans 1 affirms that all men know that God is, but they suppress that Truth in their unrighteousness. We are called on to plant the seed of His Gospel. The Lord will do the work to bring about a change in the lives of those who currently reject Him. All glory and wisdom and knowledge will be given to the Lord God Almighty.

We are maintaining that not only do Mormons not have a logically coherent answer to our argument, they cannot rationally justify their opposition to it. At the root, they have a fallible god who changes in nature, character, and ethics. The Bible, conversely, presents a perfect, holy, and unchangeable God. This God is the foundation of all intelligibility, which the LDS cannot refute. It is His Word, not human arguments, that is the test of all Truth. Not to rely on Him is to forfeit all Truth and rely on ourselves. Adam and Eve tried to rely on themselves, to be independent of God. We must strive to depend on God in all things and bring all thoughts captive to the obedience of Christ.

9

CHRISTIAN TESTIMONIES

This chapter is a collection of personal testimonies of people who have left the Mormon Church for a variety of reasons and have posted their stories on the Internet. Some of the people who wrote these letters come from strong Mormon families and are just now coming to faith in Christ. In respect of their privacy and the difficulties that they must face in leaving the Mormon Church, we will not use their actual names.

Two excellent sites for reading more testimonies are:

http://www.exmormon.org
http://www.irr.org/mit/

While reading these personal testimonies, I am constantly encouraged by the writers' desire to praise and give glory to God. More astounding are the desire to worship God as Creator and the lack of self-promoting testimony. I believe that these letters can stand on their own merit to encourage current members of the Church of Jesus Christ of Latter-day Saints to reflect on who Christ is and what we should think about Him.

As a Christian, I do not seek my own godhood; I am quite satisfied that Christ is God and serves as Mediator (1 John 1). My allegiance is to Him alone, and my faith is in Him. We are not saved through a church or any other organization. We are saved by a Savior. He who is not created has created me, and I praise Him for my salvation. He has brought me into the Kingdom of His Son and changed my life and thinking. He has given me hope and a desire to please Him. That is my testimony.

When Mormons refer to their testimony, they generally are talking about their assurance that Joseph Smith was a true Prophet and that the *Book of Mormon* is a true witness to Jesus Christ. But does this constitute a genuine testimony? The following letters are not LDS testimonies; they are Christian. They are evidence that when Christ becomes a reality in someone's life, the heart is moved to worship Him and not seek its own exaltation.

What Really Matters (Letter 1)

Dear C.,

This is what I was referring to in my last post to you. I was writing to E. about the fact that we could construct the entire New Testament from the quotations of it in letters written by the early church fathers, except for 6 verses. However, I do feel that there is a difference between saying that the Bible was incorrectly translated versus incorrectly interpreted.

Something indeed [can] be correctly translated and people can still interpret it incorrectly. That is not what the early leaders such as Orson Pratt were saying about the Bible. I believe there have been two people on *Free-Saints Now* who have told me that the 8th article of faith should really be that we believe in the Bible as far as it is correctly interpreted.

As far as the quote from 1 Nephi 13:24–30 that you gave me, I have to ask you if you are aware of the earlier manuscripts and papyri that have been discovered over the last century? These new findings take us back even closer to the original writings of the New Testament and show no changes in doctrine or parts that have been removed. The newer discoveries date back before the formation of the Catholic church, so I see no truth in the claims in 1 Nephi. The Catholic church certainly was not able to go dig up the papyri found in Egypt, erase portions of them and then rebury them! I don't want to argue with you either, C. I just hope that you can look at all the facts and decide for yourself. Remember, Jesus said, Heaven and earth shall pass away, but my words shall not pass away (Matt. 24:35). The question is, was Jesus lying when He said that? Or was He unable to fulfill that promise? Either way, if that is the case, what kind of a Savior would He be? What power would He have to atone for all of our sins?

Hello P.,

I do see your point about interpretation versus translation. Frankly, I don't pay too much attention to E. He has sent me a lot of material to read, most of which just circles the problem, without getting to the heart of the matter. I have found A. and G. to be more helpful in clarifying LDS doctrinal subjects. I have never heard that the 8th article of Faith should read "interpreted" instead of "translated." Every time this is discussed in classes that I have been in or taught, the verses in 1 Nephi 13:24–30 are also included in the instruction manual. Thus, when I think of this article of faith I associate it with the fact that in the translating process there were things that were left out. Which is entirely different than stating that the interpretation is the problem.

Actually, it no longer matters to me, because I have come to the conclusion that the prophet is false, so the Articles of Faith no longer are valid as far as I am concerned, nor anything else put forth by the prophet, which includes all things Mormon. It is still painful to say that, but I know it has to be put behind me.

Your statement that the Lord would preserve His Word and stated as much in Scripture, is something I now accept. I am finding that I am believing more in the Bible each day. My distrust of it is not even a problem anymore. And I am amazed at how quickly that distrust left once I made up my mind that the prophet was false. Also M. has recommended some books and I have been able to get several of those. These will keep me busy for a while. My head is still spinning over all of this. I never thought anything like this would happen to me. But at least I am beginning to see a course of action I can follow.

Thank you for all of your help. I will be in touch. C.

A Missionary Meets McConkie (Letter 2)

Regarding [Bruce R.] McConkie, you wrote: Yes, I sort of had the same conclusion when I asked him to autograph my

Mormon Doctrine. It was almost as if I had asked him to donate one to me. He was wearing the same tie I had on, and when I complimented his tie he sort of gave me gruff-gruff and walked away. He didn't appear to be comfortable with the troops in the pews. [One gentleman], who since his late teens has a completely cynical view of Mormondom, caught up with him and asked him if he'd seen Christ. Well, you can imagine the response. It was something like . . . ah, son, we don't talk about things like that.

For a so-called apostle, and witness, he got zero out of ten with that insipid response. It seems one can always see better with hindsight, or when looking at what others did or said, rather than at what one says or does oneself. Please understand the following comment is not intended as criticism at all, but as an "if only." . . . If only . . . someone, getting such a response from McConkie or any of the Mormon apostles, would have the presence of mind to answer, Oh! I thought that was your job! If one was willing to sacrifice the air of surprised innocence, one could even add, Paul certainly bore witness of his encounter with Christ. I guess you guys just aren't in the same class with him.

When I joined the church, I was taught that the GAs [General Authorities] met with Jesus face to face. My husband, who grew up in the church, was taught that as well. However, they seem to be sliding away from this teaching at present. Not the GAs, but the apostles, as special witnesses of Christ. Do any of the members of this list recall being taught such a thing?

Does anyone recall being told of specific instances where modern GAs spoke face to face with our Lord? John Taylor supposedly saw Christ in the upper rooms of the Salt

Lake Temple. Melvin J. Ballard supposedly had a vision or dream of Christ in which he was embraced by Him.

Bruce R. seemed full of his own importance. Exactly right. Perhaps his discomfort with the troops in the pews came from (or was augmented by) an experience he had in Salt Lake City in 1981. He was the featured guest at a wards youth conference. At the closing meeting, a Q&A session, the local Mormon missionaries were invited to join McConkie, the stake president and the bishopric on the stand, to answer questions.

It is not known if the invitation to the missionaries was actually with the thought that they would contribute answers, or simply sit as objects of admiration and aspiration whereby the glassy-eyed youth would be inspired to dream of the day when they, too, could be missionaries and, possibly, enjoy the same privilege of sharing the stand with McConkie or some other apostle. Ostensibly, the youth could ask questions of any of those on the stand, but of course none would show themselves so foolish as to ask a missionary for advice while passing the opportunity to pick the brains of the apostle, the stake president, or even the bishop.

One young man in the audience, directing his inquiry to McConkie, asked the age-old question, What is the one thing we can do as young people to most guard ourselves against temptation? (It seemed evident from his demeanor that the boy thought asking such a question was evidence he was already a spiritual giant.) McConkie gave the same age-old answer given by Joseph Fielding Smith, Spencer W. Kimball, and virtually every Mormon leader ever to write on this question: Just decide in advance there are certain things you won't do. He invited the stake president and bishop to add anything they thought appropriate, and of course they basically parroted what he had said.

One of the missionaries on the stand was familiar with this advice and had always found it frustrating. If one could decide that way in advance, he thought, then one would never even be tempted. The very nature of temptation is that one is truly considering the possibility of actually doing something wrong—shall I or shall I not? That is, one is faced with a decision, right then and there, at the moment of temptation. That cannot be decided in advance. Even if one has decided in advance that one will not do certain things, one is still faced in temptation at least with the decision, shall I stick with my earlier decision? This missionary had struggled with this issue so seriously that he thought he might have learned something worth passing on to others.

So he passed a note across to the presiding authorities and asked if he might be allowed to also address the question. With a sort of bemused indulgence, he was granted permission. He told the youth what Brigham Young had said, that all people were seeking salvation, though not all knew that is what they sought. But all desired happiness, and that is what salvation was all about. Adam fell that men might be; and men are, that they might have joy (2 Ne. 2:25).

Temptation, said the missionary, is nothing more nor less than the proposition from the world, the flesh, or the devil, that happiness can be found in things, ways, and activities that happen to be forbidden by the Lord. Sin is only man's attempt to find salvation in what cannot save, i.e., to find happiness in what will never satisfy—doing what God has forbidden or shirking what He has commanded. . . . Wickedness never was happiness (Alma 41:10). Sinful people . . . have gone contrary to the nature of God; therefore they are in a state contrary to the nature of happiness (Alma 41:11). As Helaman told the people, . . . ye have sought all the days of your lives for that which ye could not obtain; and ye have sought for happiness in doing iniquity, which thing is contrary to the nature of that righteousness which is in our great and Eternal Head (Hela. 13:38).

God, however, promises happiness and joy in doing good and following Him. He says happiness lies in one course, while the world, the flesh, and the devil suggest other courses. The missionary reasoned that, obviously, the seeker after happiness will choose his course depending upon whom he believes, or believes the most. Therefore, he thought, the key to resisting temptation, the key to resisting the proposition that happiness lies in ways apart from God, is to believe God, who promises happiness with Himself, and in His ways.

If we believe God, that is, if we trust Him, and if we are seeking happiness (as all do), then we will do what He says will make us happy. Faith in God, then, is the one thing, the most powerful weapon we have, for resisting temptation. Though some sins may be very tempting, may seem to offer happiness in immediate and powerful ways, the one who trusts God will disbelieve the promise of sin.

The missionary also posed the next two obvious questions. First, why should you trust God, when the promise of sin might be not only inviting and powerful, but to all appearances true—that is, trustworthy, able to produce the happiness it promises? His answer was that happiness was impossible apart from love. Things cannot offer love. And while some sin has the appearance of love, genuine love comes only from God. Choosing anything apart from or contrary to God only cuts us off from the true source of real love.

The missionary reasoned that we should trust God because He loves us. Second, why should we believe God loves us? The missionary said God has proven His love for us by sending Christ to die for us so we could be forgiven of our sins and return to His presence. He wants us back, and has demonstrated that love in a sacrifice of His Son which we can hardly conceive. But as we attempt to understand it, as we ponder the love that it demonstrated, we find all the reason we need to believe in God's promises and therefore act accordingly. So, not only faith in God, but faith in Christ and His atonement in particular, is our greatest weapon to resist temptation.

The above teaching was so clearly superior to McConkie's hackneyed advice that he was embarrassed. When the missionary turned to sit down, he was shocked to see McConkie's face looked both red and gray at the same time. He suddenly saw what he had never dreamed when he arose to speak, that following McConkie's remarks his own thoughts had to appear to everyone present as lacking allegiance to the teaching authority of the apostle, if not outright rebuffing or challenging him. Everyone sat speechless for a very long moment in which you could have heard a pin drop as surely as if you were in the Tabernacle.

Finally, the stake president moved to the podium. The very air was pregnant with suspense, anticipation.

The power of truth was such that some response seemed almost demanded, some comment from someone, or even a further question, inevitable. But no one could refute the missionary, and no one dared to evidence concurrence. At last in the audience a hand was raised somewhat timidly, and with evident relief the stake president called on its owner.

The questioner knew the right thing to do. Directing her question to the rather discredited apostle—and thereby demonstrating who was the real object of her faith and that of all those assembled (including the missionary)—she changed the subject to an entirely different topic. I bear you my testimony that the above story is true.

For those of you who may be wondering, the missionary did eventually leave the church and became a Christian. It seems evident that the Lord was leading him in that direction, even at this point, when he was still totally committed to Mormonism. He was struggling at that time, however, with a third question suggested by the line of reasoning he shared at that meeting, but which he did not mention there.

The question was, What does the atonement really prove about God's love for me, when He won't apply the benefit of the atonement to me for forgiveness of sins, until I have cleaned myself up and quit sinning? What kind of love is it that has made this great sacrifice for my forgiveness, but which will not actually forgive me, completely and permanently, until I conform to a standard which I find impossible to meet? How can I believe He loves me when, if I were to face Him in judgment right now, He would banish me from His presence for all eternity? God was making this missionary hungry for righteousness. At the same time, that is, by the same process, He was providing the missionary with incentive for wanting out of Mormonism, and for giving to the evidence which refutes and discredits Mormonism the weight which it deserves.

Later, after he had left Mormonism and found the real Gospel and the real Jesus, he had to conclude that the Mormon teaching about the atonement was a form of godliness which denied the power thereof (2 Tim. 3:5). With

Jesus, supposedly, and grace, mercy, and the atonement all in the picture, it still predicates forgiveness of sin on the attainment of righteousness by the one seeking forgiveness. It categorically denies that the atonement provides that righteousness itself, affirming rather that application of the atonement to the sinner's sin depends on his providing his own righteousness through repentance and good works. That is why it is powerless to save.

Hallelujah, the real Gospel, the good news, is that Jesus not only paid the debt of my sin, He also supplies all the righteousness God requires of me. Not only His death, but His life is credited to me, laid to my account as a totally free and undeserved gift, in which I trust for forgiveness of sins and full salvation.

God bless, T.

An Exit Story (Letter 3)

E.,

Yes, I have an exit story of sorts, but it's not as exciting as the others I have read. I had been unhappy in the Mormon church for some time. I was just as unhappy with most of the people in the church as I was with the doctrine. I knew some of the folks on the outside, and I knew they were not what they claimed to be when they were in church.

Not that I thought I was so great, but I didn't publicly persecute other people in efforts to make myself appear more perfect. I began asking myself questions like: Are these the type of people I want to spend eternity with? I didn't like being with them on Sundays. This really got me thinking. Do I go with these folks to heaven, or should I just give up and go on to hell? Choices like that, to me, did not seem to be what Jesus was asking us to make. I had been teaching a Sunday School class of young boys for over a year. I taught *The Articles of Faith*; I taught about the man that built the pipe organ in Salt Lake, about Joseph Smith, anything except Biblical Scripture. These 12- & 13-year-old boys didn't know the Ten Commandments but they sure knew *The Articles of Faith*.

As well, I had been watching Dr. Charles Stanley's *In Touch Ministries* on FOX television Sunday mornings for about a year. His sermons made sense. He spoke only from the Bible, and I was uplifted after hearing him. He taught of a loving, forgiving heavenly Father who promised salvation that could never be lost.

For the first time in my life I felt good about God, Jesus, and felt that maybe, just maybe there was hope for me. Maybe I could go to heaven and not be as unhappy there as I was in the LDS church.

Charles Stanley spoke about being saved. About accepting Jesus Christ as my personal Savior. So one Sunday night, in my room alone, I got down on my knees and asked Jesus if He would forgive me of all my sins. I accepted Jesus as my personal Savior. From that moment on, I have never been the same. Christ opened my eyes and I never returned to a Mormon church. That was 1988.

My parents, a brother, two sisters and their families followed that year, each at their own pace. Seventeen of us in all left the Ward within a year. Many rumors circulated about us, but we all left by the grace of Jesus Christ and were not excommunicated as rumor had it. My life did not begin until I accepted Jesus Christ of the Holy Bible.

The Bible itself, although I had read it through once, seemed to open up and the mind of God poured out of those pages.

At first I was angry at all Mormons and the church. Mormon meant enemy in my mind. I had been lied to, deceived for all of my life! Who wouldn't be angry? I had lived in absolute religious bondage. I was denied the freedom to develop a personal relationship with Jesus. I didn't even know Jesus the whole time I was a Mormon.

As time has passed God has replaced my anger at Mormon people with compassion. If I could, if God was only willing, I would devote my life to witnessing to Mormons. I hate LDS doctrine and its theology. I cringe when I see a picture of a Mormon temple. I feel frustrated that they are spiritually dead and cannot comprehend the truth. They cannot comprehend the Jesus of the Holy Bible. But all I have to do is think back. There was a time when I would argue or even fight to defend my Mormon beliefs. God has pointed out to me that the only difference between me and any Mormon is His grace.

This is why I am so grateful to Him. Jesus Christ has poured out His grace upon me, as undeserving as I am. And there are so many Mormons who are wonderful people. Why can't they experience His grace as well? This is what frustrates me.

E., this is somewhat more than an exit story. But this forum allows me a method of some healing. There are wounds from being a Mormon. I think all of us have them. Together and with the help of Jesus Christ, we will heal. I am here to do my best to help anyone I can, any way I can.

Sincerely, G.

A New Testimony (Letter 4)

Well, I found my homemade tract so you can see how it sounds:

> MY TESTIMONY
> I bear you my testimony that I know beyond a shadow of a doubt
> that Joseph Smith was a prophet, that the *Book of Mormon* is true,
> that the Church of Jesus Christ [of Latter-day Saints] is the only true Church
> upon the face of the earth today!

When I was a member of the Mormon Church, I shared this testimony with everyone I met. I was baptized a Mormon when I was fifteen years old, just in case it was the only true Church. My Mormon lineage goes back four generations. After baptism I was confirmed and given the gift of the Holy Ghost. I was not active in the Church until I was twenty-four years old after my husband was baptized in 1961.

We were both very actively engaged in genealogy work, researching and writing twelve family histories for our posterity. All twelve books are in the SLC Family History Library today. We paid our tithing and attended our church meetings faithfully, which consisted of Sacrament meeting, Priesthood and Relief Society, and the children loved their primary classes. My husband was a faithful home teacher as I was a faithful visiting teacher right up until the day I resigned.

We held regular Family Home Evenings on Monday nights with our four children and worked in all ways possible to earn our way via our good works to the top heaven, the Celestial Kingdom, where we would be gods and goddesses.

We were temple-worthy Mormons, and our names were sealed in the SLC Temple for time and all eternity along with our little children in 1962. We spent many hours doing our temple work and slaving endless hours so we could be Saviors on Mt. Zion for our departed non-Mormon loved ones.

I was a faithful worthy Mormon for thirty-two years! Then a Jehovah's Witness neighbor became concerned about me and showed me a study her Church had done on the *Book of Mormon*. Since I was witnessing to her about the Mormon Church, I allowed her equal time! She showed me that over a hundred quotations from the New Testament have been found in the first two books of Nephi alone in the *Book of Mormon*, and there were 27,000 words copied exactly from the King James Version of the Bible into that book! So her obvious question was: How can characters writing in 600 B.C. be quoting Bible sources that weren't written until six hundred years later? I really pondered what she was telling me. When I personally researched it, I came to the same conclusion; BUT since I had the burning-in-the-bosom testimony to the truthfulness of the *Book of Mormon*, I did not act upon my findings at this time. I just put them on the back burner.

On September 19, 1989, I experienced a vision on my living-room wall. It was like a slide in full technicolor! It was of the cross on Calvary. It was bent, rugged, blood-stained. But the sun was shining brightly behind it in a clear, bright blue sky! Below it was a winding path leading to the foot of the cross through autumn-colored trees. It was so beautiful! I did not know what the vision cross meant, but I took some time to sketch it. I sent the sketch to a Mormon missionary, a Navajo Indian friend, and for Christmas he sent me a carving of my vision which I still treasure today! I took the carving to Church to share my vision with everyone, but they would not look upon it! They turned their eyes from the scene and acted as if I was invisible! It was almost as if they were vampires looking upon the cross as we see in the movies. I was stunned and I was shunned. So I took it home and put it in a drawer.

On June 13, 1993, I went with my friend S. to the Chicago Temple with the Relief Society sisters. We were doing my ancestors' endowments. While in the Celestial Room my friend and I shared a bizarre experience together. In the Temple everyone gets a new name, and you are not to tell anyone except your husband what it is. So we were sitting together in the Celestial Room discussing the reverent feelings we had experienced while doing my ancestors' endowments. She started to speak to me, and MY NEW NAME came pouring out of her mouth!!! She couldn't get it to stop! Finally, I whispered in her ear that that was my new name!! And then we had a brief glimpse of everyone in the room being dressed in black! We immediately fled the Temple. We both felt that Satan was present in the Temple!

Together we decided to do an intense research on the early doctrines of the LDS Church, and we also got into a Christian Bible Study class. Later we both had dreams where Jesus or someone like Him came to us and told us that He came for the whole world and not just a select group of people! We could not figure out why we were both having these experiences. No one else seemed to have them. Why us?

One day we were reading in the Bible in Job 33:14–18, 28–30, and those verses told us why God had sent the visions and dreams to us. Although God speaks again and again, no one pays attention to what He says. At night when men are asleep, God speaks in dreams and visions, He makes them listen to what He says, and they are frightened at His warnings. God speaks to make them stop their sinning and to save them from becoming proud. (One of the pitfalls of being a Mormon is pride.) He will not let them be destroyed; He saves them from death itself—the grave, the pit. . . . He kept me from going to the world of the dead, and I am still alive. God does all this again and again; He saves a person's life and gives him the joy of living. He saved us from the pit. We finally KNEW what God was trying to tell us! WE were involved in a cult! If we continued in this cult, we would be damned!

As we faithfully studied the Bible with newly opened spiritual eyes, God opened up all the mysteries of His Kingdom to us, and we were born again, converted anew. The Third Article of the Mormon faith says, We believe that through the Atonement of Christ, all mankind may be saved, by obedience to the laws and ordinances of the Gospel. And although I was in good standing with the Church at that time, I wondered if I could ever keep the 613-plus laws just in the OT alone. In the *Book of Mormon*, I read in 2 Nephi 25:23: . . . it is by grace that we are saved, after all we can do. If I was honest with myself, neither I nor any of my LDS friends and family were really doing ALL we could do or could ever do.

As I studied the Bible, I soon desired a personal relationship with Jesus Christ, one that was forbidden to me as a member of the Mormon Church. As a Mormon I was trusting MY testimony and MY good works for salvation. I finally knelt and admitted to God that I wasn't perfect. That

I was a dirty, rotten sinner—a filthy rag (Rom. 3:23). It was very hard to do that because, as a Mormon, I was working my way toward perfection! I no longer trusted in my own good works or any church organization for eternal life. I trusted only God's Son, Jesus Christ, to save me from my sins and bring me to Heaven to live with Him as it says in Acts 4:12.

In the book *Mormon Doctrine* Bruce R. McConkie says that many people worshipping God by the right names are really worshipping false gods (p. 270). The mere worship of a god who has the proper Scriptural names does not assure one that he is worshipping the true and living God. I had worshipped all the right names in the Mormon Church, but the god was wrong. The god that I worshipped as a Latter-day Saint had a body of flesh and bone (*Doctrine and Covenants* 130:22), was a glorified, exalted man (*Gospel Through the Ages,* by Milton Hunter, p. 104), and was one of many gods (*Mormon Doctrine,* pp. 576–77).

The God of the Bible is not a man who was exalted to godhood by doing good works. Numbers 23:19 says, "God is not a man." Romans 1:22–23 says, "Professing themselves to be wise, they became fools, and changed the glory of the uncorruptible God into an image like to corruptible man." The God of the Bible is the only true God. "I am He. Before Me there was no God formed, and there will be none after Me" (Isa. 43:10). "I am the first, and I am the last; and there is no God beside Me" (Isa. 44:6). Would you believe that the *Book of Mormon* says the same thing? It agrees with the Bible in many verses and disagrees with the doctrine as the Mormon Church teaches it today.

I now believe that the *Book of Mormon* is a 19th-century book written by Joseph Smith to get gain and fame, and that it was copied from the King James Bible which he owned and several other books available in that day like the *View of the Hebrews*, etc. The New Testament is even quoted in many places such as Alma, Moroni, etc. Thus the doctrine of Jesus Christ is taught in the *Book of Mormon* in about 559–545 B.C. long before Christ Himself taught it!

I now realize that many false religions and cults perform the same rituals and ceremonies that the Church of Jesus Christ of Latter-day Saints does. I resigned from that Church in March 1994 and joined and was re-baptized in the First Christian Church, and later rejoined the Lutheran Church where I was married. According to the Bible, the only true Gospel is that Christ died on the cross, like the one in my vision, for my sins, was buried, and rose again for my personal salvation (1 Cor. 15:1–4). I thought I could earn my way to Celestial Exaltation, but what I really needed was to trust Jesus Christ alone as my Savior. Ephesians 2:8–9 says: "For by grace are ye saved through faith; and that not of yourselves: it is the gift of God; not of works, lest any man should boast." I would urge anyone who reads this tract to come to the God of the Bible, the only true God (Deut. 4:35). He loves you and sent His Son, Jesus Christ, to die for your sins. "God has given us eternal life, and this life is in His Son. He who has the Son has life; he who does not have the Son of God does not have the life" (1 John 5:11–12).

My new testimony is this: I KNOW beyond a shadow of a doubt that Jesus is the Christ and Savior of the world. That He died for my sins and was resurrected. I KNOW that I am saved by grace and not by works and will inherit heaven upon that principle. I also KNOW that God hears and answers prayers. I KNOW all this not only by the feeling I have from the inner witness of the Holy Spirit but by the reliability of God's Word, the Holy Bible, His love letter to me. And, I also KNOW that because of my relationship with Jesus Christ, He has changed my life and continues to bless me.

I hope this doesn't bore you! Some people aren't too religious after leaving a cult and don't want to have anything to do with any religion. But I didn't have that problem, thank goodness, although the Christian churches don't seem to have as much fun as I did as a Mormon. They are more dry! But I still feel God's presence in them!

SIMILAR TESTIMONIES (LETTER 5)

The following are testimonies of subjective experiences that verified truth:

Moriah, who is still firm in the faith (Jewish background), is 26 and has been exploring many religions since she was 16. She says, I've been looking for something for a long time and didn't know what I should do. What they had to say just felt right. My head told me that their story didn't make sense, but I had a strong inner feeling that told me, Hey, you've got to do this.

Levi, 20, was raised a Catholic in the Midwest. He found members of the group and says, I felt they were sincere, truth-seeking, happy and fulfilled. For the first time in my life, I have a firm faith that there is something higher.

David, who is 33, was willing to leave a mistress he was really fond of. He was raised Catholic, but went over to agnosticism when young. He attended a meeting and there he felt a great surge of energy that meant that this message was meant for him.

It's amazing how much impact a subjective testimony can have. None of these testimonies are that unique—they could have come from the *Ensign*, "Missionary Moments" in the *Church News* or even a fireside meeting. But they don't. These testimonies come from followers of Marshall Applegate and the Heaven's Gate group that recently committed suicide in San Diego. The interviews were part of an article done by the *New York Times* on Feb. 29, 1976, and called "Looking For: The Next World" by James S. Phelan, that we pulled off the Internet.

Scary, isn't it?

Leaning hard on Him who is the Truth, J.

Working for Salvation (Letter 6)

Well, P., I went up pretty high in the church. I think some confusion comes about because we have Mormons who are at various levels, and it is only as you go higher that the pressure truly increases.

For example, when I taught Spiritual Living in my ward, of course I had to act and have a family that seemed perfect. My best friends were stake leaders, and I was invited onto more and more stake, then finally regional, committees. We sisters who got higher and higher were usually assigned to home teach each other, because those lower down couldn't possibly know the pressures that we were under.

We worked as hard as any Bishop in certain callings, such as Stake Relief Society Counselor or, in my case, Regional Historian, and also I was a Regional Publicity Director in charge of all the church publicity for several states. I rolled right along, secure in my calling and in a sense of righteousness, sure that I was progressing, confident of my status as an elect Lady. I received a certificate stating that I was an elect Lady, and received a great deal of support from equally dedicated and perpetually exhausted women, all of us with what seemed to be ideal, well-balanced lives and families.

I dutifully followed ALL the laws, but at interview time, one question always got me stumped: I was actually asked if I had EVER sinned against anyone knowingly, and I was expected to answer in the negative to get my Temple recommend renewed. I was in annual agony over it and well knew I had sinned here, there and everywhere in many minor ways. I would just have to keep on trying harder! Harder!

I watched my dear friends become driving robots, almost destroying themselves, not daring to admit they were losing important battles within. What were we losing? We got to the point of not caring, just burning out. We consoled each other with stories about spiritual dreams we'd had, or genuine encounters with good or evil beings. We often seemed to have visions or were in the center of unexplainable coincidences, but in most cases, we thanked God for OUR actions.

We rarely saw the Lord in action: WE were the ones challenged to choose righteously, to do righteously. Righteousness was the name of the game. Then Jesus appeared to me in a dream. I was wearing my Temple garments, which I saw were but filthy rags! And He said to me in great patience, with a voice that rang through my entire being: I AM YOUR COVERING. I, myself, now know that it is only by the grace of God that I, a sinner, have been saved. Jesus' great mercy showed me who I was.

I am proud to be known as a Christian. I am not righteous; Christ covers me, and in HIS righteousness, I am secure. Mormons, alas, must forever extend their righteous actions, their work, their labors. There is only more of the same for them: unremitting toil, labor . . . and then, when they're all worn out, they get to hear the song: . . . DO something MORE! . . . Doing good is a pleasure, a joy beyond measure. . . . [The world] has no use for the DRONE! DRONES are worthless in the beehive and are kicked out to die, you know . . . a sort of religious *Animal Farm* theme. . . . Well, I hope this is some help. . . . If you're lower down, you're basically taught less, expected to do less, unless they decide you're worth breaking in to the harness.

In His Name, J.

Mormonism Goes Public (Letter 7)

Dear K.,

The LDS church simply isn't what it advertises itself to be. All the slick commercials you see are just that, marketing aimed at increasing market share in the form of membership.

Being a Mormon means engaging in a life of learning and dispensing one side of an issue, the side that favors the church. Much like a salesman who doesn't tell you the bad things about his product, he only tells you the superficial good things. After you've made your purchase (baptism), you begin reading the fine print. The fine print is constantly being made smaller by your fellow Mormons who tell you not to read the fine print. Reading the fine print is bad; you're a bad person if you actually learn what you're getting yourself into.

Hand in hand with its marketing, the LDS church is engaged in a continuous, systematic campaign to keep its public image intact at all costs. Unfortunately, the church's image is more important than the lives, good names, and reputations of its members. The church stifles and suppresses any bad news about itself. It spins or revises its own history and doctrine to satisfy whatever audience it is trying to influence.

After 34 years as an active Mormon, I could finally no longer ignore the fact that the LDS church has a whole heap of serious problems which can only be alleviated if the church as a body repents of its dubious past and present, and starts being honest with its members and the rest of the Christian community. The church has suspended or abandoned many of its former quaint quirky beliefs and practices, but it has not repudiated them.

The church leaders are attempting to sit astride a fence—trying to become part of mainstream Christianity while simultaneously appeasing old-line members who still remember being taught differently. Mormons as a whole are honest and conscientious but, who, because of the doctrine of the infallibility of the prophet, are kept in a state of spiritual frustration. They are told to follow the brethren: When the brethren speak, the thinking has been done. I believe those of us who have elected to leave have tired of allowing someone else to do our thinking.

We are tired of being told what to wear, whom to associate with, what to read, where to be, and a hundred other have-to's. If Mormonism were a social club, I'd enjoy it. I have many lifelong friends in the church, and I am losing those friends because of leaving the church. Friday night . . . my daughter babysat the bishop's kids. The bishop told her, We miss you at church. My daughter said, We've been busy. (Didn't have the heart to tell him we've been busy going to another church.)

If the church would repudiate its past, and make significant strides towards true Christianity, I'd go back next week. But I don't know if the church is capable of doing that.

AFTERWORD

Studies on the topic of Mormonism range from general introductions through specific theological issues. In many studies, I have noticed that the authors tend to spout too much personal opinion and ignore primary source material. I hope that this study will aid the reader in digging deeper into Scripture to find the Truth about the matters that have been raised.

I have spoken to members of the Church of Jesus Christ of Latter-day Saints in depth. At the end of those discussions I run into one theme. At some point, the person to whom I am speaking will tell me that the final proof of the *Book of Mormon* and the LDS Church rests solely on the test from Moroni 10:4–5:

> And when ye shall receive these things, I would exhort you that ye would ask God, the Eternal Father, in the name of Christ, if these things are not true; and if ye shall ask with a sincere heart, with real

> intent, having faith in Christ, he will manifest the truth of it unto you, by the power of the Holy Ghost. And by the power of the Holy Ghost ye may know the truth of all things.

This is the final test for the Mormon. However, as I stated in the beginning, all of us, Christians and non-Christians alike, are told to examine the words of men. This is not testing God. Faith is called for. When we are presented with a word that claims to be from God, it must be put to the test of His Word.

Moroni 10:4–5 is a subjective test based on logical fallacies. To follow the logic of the verses, when I read the *Book of Mormon,* I should pray to God to reveal if it is true. If one were an atheist and did not believe in God, why would one pray to God? The test presupposes faith in Him. If I do have faith in Christ, He will, presumably, reveal the truth of the *Book of Mormon* to me. This begs the question whether it is true or not. Maybe when I pray, God will reveal the falsity of the *Book of Mormon;* certainly this is a possibility, but Moroni does not leave room for that possibility. The reader who still does not believe the *Book of Mormon* to be true is left to wonder:

1. If the Holy Ghost has not revealed to me that the *Book of Mormon* is true, why not?
2. If the Holy Spirit has not revealed this to me, is it possible that I do not have the ability to discover the truth in all things?

One Mormon friend of mine told me, "When I discovered the truth of the *Book of Mormon,* I felt like running around and telling everyone how I felt and what I knew to be true." Well, when children find out about the Easter Bunny, they get a little excited too. I know that this illustration might seem offensive, but my point is that personal experience proves nothing. If I believed in Communism, that would not make Communism the correct form of government. A system that may seem to work is not necessarily true, nor does believing or feeling that something is true make it so.

My ultimate hope for this study is that the reader may be better equipped to present the Gospel to a Mormon follower. Paul was not ignorant of the Greeks when he spoke to them. He knew of their false deities. In a similar manner, a general understanding of LDS doctrine is essential in speaking to a member of the Church of Jesus Christ of Latter-day Saints. Keep in mind that Christianity is not well served by blind followers. Even though one may be familiar with LDS theology in order to witness to Mormons more effectively, there is no substitute for knowing the truths taught in the Bible.

Understanding the doctrinal differences between Christianity and Mormonism is extremely important. I would suggest that a person speaking to a Mormon not start the conversation by debating different points of doctrine, though that is important. But starting with the Gospel and salvation in Christ will help direct the conversation to what is central to any discussion of religious matters. Mormon missionaries generally have short, one-line answers for many questions that non-Mormons ask. Most of them are not prepared to discuss the heart of the Gospel from Scripture. Their presentations are carefully scripted by their Church leaders. They know what their Church teaches, and they know what they are expected to say to the people to whom they are witnessing. Ask them to back up what they say with Scripture. Do not accept a subjective test of truth. Read Scripture in context, and challenge your Mormon friend to do the same.

Let me clarify my point by illustration. Imagine a child's swing-set in a park or in a backyard. View the disputed points of doctrine as the swings that are supported by the large stabilizing bars. The Gospel and the issue of salvation through Christ are like those large bars. The swings, that is, the individual doctrines, while important, point to the strength of the supporting bars (the true Gospel). In other words, without a proper understanding of the Gospel, the individual doctrines become irrelevant in any further discussions. Without a biblical understanding of Christ and the Gospel, the individual doctrines of the LDS Church cannot be supported.

NOTES

Chapter 1: Setting the Stage

1. "Unbelief," in *Journal of Discourses*, 18 May 1873 (Salt Lake City: Deseret, 1994), 16:46–47.

2. Joseph Fielding Smith, Introduction to *Answers to Gospel Questions* (Salt Lake City: Deseret, 1994), 2:xiii.

3. Ezra Taft Benson, "Gospel Principles and Doctrines," in *Teachings of Ezra Taft Benson* (Salt Lake City: Deseret, 1994), 1:57.

4. Heber J. Grant, "Living Our Religion," in *Gospel Standards* (Salt Lake City: Deseret, 1994), 1:47.

5. "Our Fellow Men," in *Discourses of Brigham Young* (Salt Lake City: Deseret, 1994), 278.

6. Spencer W. Kimball, "Forgive to Be Forgiven," in *Miracle of Forgiveness* (Salt Lake City: Deseret, 1994), 275.

7. Ezra Taft Benson, "The Church," in *Teachings of Ezra Taft Benson*, 2:212.

8. "Nebuchadnezzar's Dream," in *Journal of Discourses*, 26 July 1857, 5:73.

9. "The United States Administration and Utah Army," in *Journal of Discourses*, 13 Sept. 1857, 5:229.

10. "Civilization-Missionary Labours," in *Journal of Discourses,* 16 Sept. 1860, 8:171.

11. "Persecution—The Kingdom of God," in *Journal of Discourses,* 7 Oct. 1860, 8:199.

12. "Judgment According to Works," in *Journal of Discourses,* 17 Jan. 1858, 6:176.

13. Also, take notice of the slanderous accusation about the integrity of Christians.

14. John Taylor, "Blessings of the Saints," in *Journal of Discourses,* 17 Jan. 1858, 6:167.

15. John Taylor, "The Kingdom of God or Nothing," in *Journal of Discourses,* 1 Nov. 1857, 6:25.

16. John Taylor, "How to Know the Things of God," in *Journal of Discourses,* 6 May 1870, 13:225.

17. Bruce R. McConkie, *Mormon Doctrine* (Salt Lake City: Bookcraft, 1979), 513. This one-volume dictionary of terms used within the LDS Church affords valuable insight into Mormon doctrine. Many Mormons, however, do not accept this work as authoritative because McConkie was not a Prophet of the Church, but one of its twelve Apostles.

18. Church of Jesus Christ of Latter-day Saints, *History of the Church,* 7 vols. (Salt Lake City: Deseret, 1980), 1:4. This compilation of historical accounts has been edited by consecutive leaders within the LDS community. The history purports to contain the actual diaries of Joseph Smith. Jerald and Sandra Tanner (*Mormonism: Shadow or Reality?* [Salt Lake City: Utah Lighthouse Ministry, 1987]) have done extensive research to show that approximately 60 percent of the *History* was written after Joseph Smith's death and cannot be construed as Smith's own words.

19. *History,* 1:5. This reference claims that Joseph Smith saw God the Father and lived.

20. *History,* 1:11. Although many LDS authorities believe that the ancient Americans in fact lived in Central America, Joseph Smith claimed that the Hill Cumorah was actually in New York. A compilation of archaeological research available from the Tanners at Utah Lighthouse Ministry disproves such claims for both North and Central America.

21. McConkie, *Mormon Doctrine,* 175.

22. Gordon B. Hinckley, *Truth Restored* (Salt Lake City: Deseret, 1979), 32–33. As the Sustained President of the Church since May 1995, Hinckley has the authority to make and correct official doctrine.

23. Joseph Fielding Smith, *Doctrines of Salvation,* 3 vols. (Salt Lake City: Bookcraft, 1954–56), 1:189.

24. Robert A. Morey, *How to Answer a Mormon* (Minneapolis: Bethany House, 1983), 16, 18.

25. James E. Talmage, *Articles of Faith* (Salt Lake City: Deseret, 1984), 8.

26. Morey, *How to Answer a Mormon,* 18.

27. Talmage, *Articles of Faith,* 7.

28. Bill McKeever and Eric Johnson, *Questions to Ask Your Mormon Friend* (Minneapolis: Bethany House, 1994), 37.

29. The Church of Jesus Christ of Latter-day Saints, *Gospel Principles* (Salt Lake City: Deseret, 1978), 47, 49–50.

30. Joseph Fielding Smith, "Israel: God's Covenant People," in *Doctrines of Salvation* (Salt Lake City: Deseret, 1994), 3:255.

31. Joseph Fielding Smith, "Biblical Evidence That Joseph Smith Was Called of God," in *Answers to Gospel Questions,* vol. 3, chap. 2, p. 12.

32. Harold B. Lee, "The Mission of the Church Schools," in *Ye Are the Light of the World* (Salt Lake City: Deseret, 1994), 104.

33. Spencer W. Kimball, "God Will Forgive," in *Miracle of Forgiveness,* 349.

34. Benson, "The Church," 2:169.

35. John Ankerberg and John Weldon, *Everything You Ever Wanted to Know About Mormonism* (Eugene, Ore.: Harvest House, 1992), 67–68.

CHAPTER 2: THE STANDARD WORKS

1. *Doctrine and Covenants* 20:8–9.

2. James E. Talmage, *Articles of Faith* (Salt Lake City: Deseret, 1984), art. 8.

3. *Doctrine and Covenants* 42:12.

4. *Doctrine and Covenants* 135:3.

5. Joseph Smith, *History of the Church of Jesus Christ of Latter-day Saints,* 7 vols. (Salt Lake City: Deseret, 1976), 4:461. However the author's name may appear on different revisions of the *History,* it has been well documented that a majority of the *History* was not written by Joseph Smith. Later editors deleted many statements and inserted new material to

clean up what Joseph had originally written. See Jerald and Sandra Tanner, *Mormonism: Shadow or Reality?* (Salt Lake City: Utah Lighthouse Ministry, 1987).

6. For a thorough demonstration of the revisions that appeared in the later version *(Doctrine and Covenants)*, see Tanner and Tanner, *Mormonism*. See also their work *Flaws in the Pearl of Great Price* (Salt Lake City: Utah Lighthouse Ministry, n.d.). Former members of the Mormon Church, Jerald and Sandra converted and started a ministry to extend the Gospel of Jesus Christ to those still within the LDS Church. Many Mormons are told that the Tanners are hateful and are in league with Satan. These ad hominem attacks to discredit the work that the Tanners have done have not stopped their ministry. Their writings are well documented, built on both primary and secondary sources, and are highly reliable.

7. Tanner and Tanner, *Mormonism*, 374. The quote is from "Spiritual Gifts," in *Pamphlets* by Orson Pratt, p. 75. Pratt was an early Apostle of the Mormon Church.

8. *Doctrine and Covenants* 42:12.

9. *Gospel Principles* (Salt Lake City: Deseret, 1979), 49. (This title is distributed by the LDS Church for Sunday school teaching material.)

10. Joseph Fielding Smith, *Doctrines of Salvation*, 3 vols. (Salt Lake City: Bookcraft, 1954–56), 1:322.

11. The *Book of Mormon* is sometimes referred to as "another testament" of Jesus Christ.

12. Joseph Smith, *Teachings of the Prophet Joseph Smith* (Salt Lake City: Deseret, 1976), 327.

13. "The Eighth Article of Faith," in *The Pearl of Great Price* (Salt Lake City: The Church of Jesus Christ of Latter-day Saints, 1989).

14. LDS Apostle Orson Pratt claimed that the Bible is in a "corrupted state" and has been "mutilated, changed and corrupted in such a shameful manner that no two manuscripts agree" (*Divine Authenticity of the Book of Mormon*, 47).

15. This observation was made by Lane Thuet in personal correspondence.

16. Bruce R. McConkie, *Mormon Doctrine* (Salt Lake City: Bookcraft, 1979), 98–99, quoting Joseph Smith.

17. *Doctrine and Covenants* 68:4.

18. Joseph Fielding Smith, *Answers to Gospel Questions* (Salt Lake City: Deseret, 1958), 2:202.

19. McConkie, *Mormon Doctrine,* 563.

20. Talmage, *Articles of Faith,* 6–7.

Chapter 3: The Mormon Gospel

1. To avoid the criticism that we are quoting "corrupted" Bible versions, our quotations of the King James are taken from *The Official Scriptures of The Church of Jesus Christ of Latter-day Saints* (Salt Lake City: Intellectual Reserve, Inc., 2000).

2. James E. Talmage, "Baptism for the Dead," in *Articles of Faith,* Deseret Book® LDS Internet Library, 136.

3. For the laws and ordinances of the Gospel, see pp. 46–47.

4. Talmage, "Faith," in *Articles of Faith,* 98.

5. Talmage, in *Articles of Faith,* Appendix 5:2, notes.

6. George Q. Cannon, "Baptism," in *Gospel Truth,* Deseret Book® LDS Internet Library, 135.

7. Wilford Woodruff, in *Journal of Discourses,* 4:192.

8. Joseph F. Smith, "Eternal Life and Salvation," in *Gospel Doctrine,* Deseret Book® LDS Internet Library, 441.

9. Joseph F. Smith, "The First Principles of the Gospel," in *Gospel Doctrine,* 96–97.

10. Ibid.

11. *Doctrine and Covenants* section 89, known as the Word of Wisdom, is regarded by members of the LDS Church as a revelation from God. It prohibits the consumption of wine, strong drink, tobacco, hot drinks, and the flesh of beasts and fowl of the air (except in winter, cold, or famine). Yet one has only to turn to volumes 2, 5, and 6 of the *History of the [LDS] Church* to find many references to Joseph Smith's use of wine and beer (though only in older versions of the *History,* as some references have since been removed). Ironically, the first LDS Prophet continued to own a bar even after he had revealed this will and command of God regarding the prohibition of alcohol. One might also search the *Journal of Discourses,* where Brigham Young often gives details about his whiskey distillery in Salt Lake City and his consumption of tea and tobacco on a very regular basis. It was quite the capitalistic enterprise for the LDS in Utah.

12. It is noteworthy that while receiving the Holy Ghost is considered an "ordinance" of the Lord, partaking of the sacrament is not. The sacrament prescribed by Christ as the Lord's Supper, consisting of wine and bread, differs from the sacrament in the LDS Church. Their sacrament consists of water and bread.

13. *Gospel Principles* (Salt Lake City: The Church of Jesus Christ of Latter-day Saints, 1990), 291–92.

14. *Discourses of Brigham Young: The Gospel Defined,* ed. John A. Widtsoe (1941), Deseret Book® LDS Internet Library, 1.

15. Ibid.

16. *Journal of Discourses,* 4:219, 220.

17. By Brigham Young and Heber C. Kimball in *Journal of Discourses,* 1:108–9, 3:226, 4:53–54, 4:375, and 10:110. It is stated in *Doctrine and Covenants* 132:26 and by Joseph Smith in *History of the Church,* 5:296. It is also taught by Joseph Fielding Smith in *Doctrines of Salvation,* 1:133.

18. *Gospel Principles* (Salt Lake City: The Church of Jesus Christ of Latter-day Saints, 1979), 66.

19. Bill McKeever, *Calvary or Gethsemane? The Atonement According to Mormonism,* http://www.mrm.org/articles/atonement.html

20. John Owen, *The Death of Death in the Death of Christ* (London: Banner of Truth Trust, 1989), 46–47.

21. Ibid., 47.

22. The LDS doctrine of God will be discussed in chap. 4.

23. *Doctrine and Covenants* 132:37, Deseret Book® LDS Internet Library.

24. The doctrine of God and the plurality of gods will be covered in chap. 4.

25. Joseph Smith, *Teachings of the Prophet Joseph Smith* (Salt Lake City: Church of Jesus Christ of Latter-day Saints, 1842–43); Deseret Book® LDS Internet Library, section 5, pp. 265–66.

26. Joseph Smith, *Lectures on Faith,* lecture 7, Deseret Book® LDS Internet Library, 7:17.

27. For examples of this assertion see especially the discussion of the Adam-God doctrine, pp. 98–111.

28. A footnote in the LDS version of the King James for Romans 3:28 gives an alternate meaning for the Greek word translated "without," namely, "apart from, without intervention of." Strange, then, that the

LDS Prophets quoted so far are so adamant about being saved by obedience to the law, when their study notes indicate that salvation is "apart from" works.

Chapter 4: Mormonism's Doctrine of God

1. The point has been made to this author numerous times that the combination of nineteenth-century social events and the lack of knowledge concerning church history has been the leading force behind the rise of over thirty prominent cultic groups in the United States in the mid 1800s.

2. Bruce R. McConkie, *Mormon Doctrine* (Salt Lake City: Bookcraft, 1979), 576–77.

3. *Doctrine and Covenants* 121:28.

4. *Doctrine and Covenants* 121:32.

5. *Articles of Faith* (Salt Lake City: Deseret, 1984), chap. notes, p. 466.

6. *Journal of Discourses,* 7:333.

7. Journal of Wilford Woodruff, 10 Apr. 1852.

8. *Journal of Discourses,* 3:109.

9. Joseph Smith, lecture 5, in "On Faith," in *Doctrine and Covenants,* 1835 edition, 52–54.

10. "The Testimony of the Three Witnesses," in the Introduction to the *Book of Mormon.*

11. *Doctrine and Covenants* 130:22.

12. McConkie, *Mormon Doctrine,* 318–19.

13. Joseph Smith, *Journal of Discourses,* 6:3.

14. *Journal of Discourses,* 4:192.

15. From an interview with Gordon B. Hinckley, 4 Aug. 1997, in *The Empire of the Mormons* (New York: Time-Life, 1997), 56.

Chapter 5: Baptism for the Dead and the Origin of Sin

1. James E. Talmage, *Articles of Faith* (Salt Lake City: Deseret, 1984), 131.

2. Ibid., 133.

3. *Gospel Principles* (Salt Lake City: Deseret, 1978), 248.

4. LeGrand Richards, *A Marvelous Work and a Wonder* (Salt Lake City: Deseret, 1958), 177.

5. *Doctrine and Covenants* 124:29.

6. *History of the Church*, 7 vols. (Salt Lake City: Deseret, 1980), 2:xxx (introduction).

7. Moses 7:38–39.

8. John Widtsoe, *Joseph Smith—Seeker After Truth* (Salt Lake City: Bookcraft, 1957), 178.

9. Talmage, *Articles of Faith*, 134.

10. Alma 34:34–35.

11. 2 Nephi 9:38.

12. Matthew Henry, *Commentary on the Holy Bible*, 6 vols. (Grand Rapids: Baker, 1960 reprint), 6:1321.

13. Jacob 6:10.

14. Alma 5:56–57.

15. Bruce R. McConkie, *Mormon Doctrine* (Salt Lake City: Bookcraft, 1979), 735.

16. Moses 5:11.

17. 2 Nephi 2:22–23.

18. Concerning the nature of man, Brigham Young claimed that the Apostle Paul was mistaken in 1 Corinthians 2. The LDS Prophet Young claimed that "unnatural man" does not receive the things of God and "the natural man is of God" (*Journal of Discourses*, 9:305; Young makes a similar assertion in 10:189; the same thought is echoed in Mosiah 3:19 and by Prophet John Taylor in *Journal of Discourses*, 10:50).

19. Moses 6:54–55.

Chapter 6: Creation and Adam

1. Bruce R. McConkie, *Mormon Doctrine* (Salt Lake City: Bookcraft, 1979), 589.

2. Brigham Young, *Deseret Weekly News*, 18 June 1873. Copies of this newspaper can be purchased for a minimal charge from Utah Lighthouse Ministry (P.O. Box 1884, Salt Lake City, UT 84110).

3. Ibid.

4. Joseph Smith, *History of the Church*, 7 vols. (Salt Lake City: Deseret, 1980), 3:386–87.

5. I am indebted to Lane Thuet for this observation and reference.

6. Young, *Deseret Weekly News*, 18 June 1873.

7. *Journal of Discourses,* 1:50–51, as cited by Jerald and Sandra Tanner in *LDS Apostle Confesses Brigham Young Taught Adam-God Doctrine* (Salt Lake City: Utah Lighthouse Ministry, 1982), 2.

8. Wilford Woodruff, private journal, 19 Feb. 1854, photocopy courtesy of the Tanners.

9. Ibid., 17 Sept. 1854.

10. Ibid., 16 Dec. 1869.

11. Brigham Young, handwritten address, 19 Feb. 1854, in LDS Church Archives, Brigham Young Papers, Ms f, #81, p. 7, photocopy courtesy of the Tanners.

12. Brigham Young, handwritten address, 8 Oct. 1854, in Brigham Young Papers, Ms d, 1234, photocopy courtesy of the Tanners.

13. Orson Pratt, record of the meeting of the Council of the Twelve, 5 Apr. 1860, photocopy courtesy of the Tanners.

14. Tanner and Tanner, *LDS Apostle,* 3.

15. Ibid.

16. Pratt, record of the Council of the Twelve, 5 Apr. 1860, reproduced in Tanner and Tanner, *LDS Apostle,* part 3.

17. George Q. Cannon, in the Proceedings of the First Sunday School Convention of the Church of Jesus Christ of Latter-day Saints, Salt Lake City, 1899, reproduced in Jerald and Sandra Tanner, *Mormonism: Shadow or Reality?* (Salt Lake City: Utah Lighthouse Ministry, 1987), 178.

18. LeGrand Richards, personal letter, 11 May 1966, quoted in Tanner and Tanner, *Mormonism,* 178.

19. Hugh Brown, personal letter, 13 May 1966, quoted in Tanner and Tanner, *LDS Apostle.*

20. Joseph Fielding Smith, *Answers to Gospel Questions* (Salt Lake City: Deseret, 1966), 5:123.

21. Spencer W. Kimball, Conference Speech, 2 Oct. 1976, reported in *Deseret News,* Church Section, 9 Oct. 1976.

22. Bruce R. McConkie, personal letter to Eugene England, 19 Feb. 1981, p. 6, reproduced in Tanner and Tanner, *LDS Apostle,* part 2.

23. Ibid., 4.

24. Ibid., 7.

25. *Journal of Discourses,* 1:50–51.

Chapter 7: The *Book of Mormon* and the Bible

1. James E. Talmage, *Articles of Faith* (Salt Lake City: Deseret, 1984), 247.

2. Bruce R. McConkie, *Mormon Doctrine* (Salt Lake City: Bookcraft, 1979), 765.

3. An interesting piece of information was forwarded to the author before publication, which claims that Joseph Smith never actually "translated" any part of the Bible as many LDS believe. "Smith never referred to any ancient texts and applied himself to translating from ancient languages to English. He simply read through his King James Version of the Bible and made changes by 'inspiration.' The LDS are wrong to assume that their version of the Old and New Testament is a translation. The Reorganized Church of Jesus Christ of Latter-day Saints, conversely, recognize this point and correctly call their Bible the 'Inspired Version of the Bible.' "

4. Joseph Fielding Smith, *Answers to Gospel Questions* (Salt Lake City: Deseret, 1958), 2:207.

5. *History of the Church*, 7 vols. (Salt Lake City: Deseret, 1980), 1:368.

6. Talmage, *Articles of Faith*, 502.

7. 1 Nephi 13:26.

8. *Doctrine and Covenants* 20:8–9.

9. *Doctrine and Covenants* 27:5.

10. *Doctrine and Covenants* 35:17.

11. *Doctrine and Covenants* 42:12.

12. It is interesting to note that the *Book of Mormon's* alternate title "Another Testament" does have at least one biblical reference: Galatians 1:6–10.

Chapter 8: The Ethical Argument Against Mormonism

1. R. C. Sproul, *Now That's a Good Question* (Wheaton, Ill.: Tyndale House Publishers, 1996), 511–12. Sproul is professor of theology at Knox Theological Seminary and Westminster Theological Seminary.

2. Bruce R. McConkie, *Mormon Doctrine* (Salt Lake City: Bookcraft, 1979), 578.

3. *Journal of Discourses*, 21:9–10.

4. McConkie, *Mormon Doctrine*, 578.

BOOKS FOR FURTHER STUDY

Anderson, Einar. *Inside Story of Mormonism.* Grand Rapids: Kregel, 1973.

Ankerberg, John, and John Weldon. *Everything You Ever Wanted to Know About Mormonism.* Eugene, Ore.: Harvest House, 1992.

Cowan, Marvin W. *Mormon Claims Answered.* Salt Lake City: Marvin W. Cowan, 1973.

Lewis, Gordon R. *The Bible, the Christian, and Latter-day Saints.* Phillipsburg, New Jersey: Presbyterian and Reformed, 1966.

McKeever, Bill. *Answering Mormons' Questions.* Minneapolis: Bethany House, 1991.

McKeever, Bill, and Eric Johnson. *Questions to Ask Your Mormon Friend.* Minneapolis: Bethany House, 1994.

Morey, Robert A. *How to Answer a Mormon.* Minneapolis: Bethany House, 1983.

Scott, Latayne Colvett. *The Mormon Mirage.* Grand Rapids: Zondervan, 1979.

Sproul, R. C. *Essential Truths of the Christian Faith.* Wheaton, Ill.: Tyndale, 1992.

———. *Grace Unknown.* Grand Rapids: Baker, 1997.

Tanner, Jerald and Sandra. *The Changing World of Mormonism.* Chicago: Moody, 1980.

WORKS OF MORMON PROPHETS

JOSEPH SMITH

The Church of Jesus Christ of Latter-day Saints: History of the Church. 7 vols. Salt Lake City: Deseret, 1980.

Teachings of the Prophet Joseph Smith: Selected and Arranged by the Historian Joseph Fielding Smith and His Assistants in the Historian's Office of the Church of Jesus Christ of Latter-day Saints. Salt Lake City: Deseret, 1976.

BRIGHAM YOUNG

"Blessings of the Saints" (1858). In *Journal of Discourses,* vol. 6.

"Civilization-Missionary Labour" (1860). In *Journal of Discourses,* vol. 5.

Discourses of Brigham Young . . . Selected and Arranged by John A. Widtsoe. Salt Lake City: Deseret, 1925.

Journal of Discourses: By Brigham Young, His Two Counsellors, the Twelve Apostles, and Others: Reported by G. D. Watt. Liverpool: F. D. Richards, 1854.

"Judgment According to Works" (1858). In *Journal of Discourses,* vol. 6.
"Nebuchadnezzar's Dream" (1857). In *Journal of Discourses,* vol. 5.
"Our Fellow Men." In *Discourses of Brigham Young.*
"Persecution—The Kingdom of God" (1860). In *Journal of Discourses,* vol. 5.
"Unbelief" (1873). In *Journal of Discourses,* vol. 16.
"The United States Administration and Utah Army" (1857). In *Journal of Discourses,* vol. 5.

JOHN TAYLOR
"How to Know the Things of God" (1870). In *Journal of Discourses,* vol. 6.
"The Kingdom of God or Nothing" (1857). In *Journal of Discourses,* vol. 6.

HEBER J. GRANT
Gospel Standards: Selections from the Sermons and Writings of Heber J. Grant. Salt Lake City: The Improvement, 1941.
"Living Our Religion." In *Gospel Standards,* vol. 1.

JOSEPH FIELDING SMITH
Answers to Gospel Questions. 5 vols. Salt Lake City: Deseret, 1957–66.
"Biblical Evidence That Joseph Smith Was Called of God." In *Answers to Gospel Questions,* vol. 3.
Doctrines of Salvation: Sermons and Writings. Compiled by Bruce R. McConkie. 3 vols. Salt Lake City: Bookcraft, 1954–56.
"Israel: God's Covenant People." In *Doctrines of Salvation,* vol. 3.

HAROLD B. LEE
"The Mission of the Church Schools." In *Ye Are the Light of the World.*
Ye Are the Light of the World: Selected Sermons and Writings of President Harold B. Lee. Salt Lake City: Deseret, 1974.

SPENCER W. KIMBALL
The Miracle of Forgiveness. Salt Lake City: Bookcraft, 1969.

EZRA TAFT BENSON
"The Church." In *The Teachings of Ezra Taft Benson,* vol. 2.
Gospel Principles. Salt Lake City: Deseret, 1978.
The Teachings of Ezra Taft Benson. 2 vols. Salt Lake City: Bookcraft, 1988.

GORDON B. HINCKLEY
Gospel Principles. Salt Lake City: Deseret, 1978.
Truth Restored. Salt Lake City: Deseret, 1979.

INDEX OF SCRIPTURE

INDEX OF PERSONS

Ethan E. Harris (B.A., Th.M.) served as resource consultant and director of conferencing at Ligonier Ministries for five years, following eight years' service in the U.S. Army.

An encounter with a Mormon in the Army National Guard launched Harris on this study and analysis of Mormon theology. Extensive contact with members of the Church of Jesus Christ of Latter-day Saints since then has exposed him to many Mormon teachings and arguments.

His thorough attention to official publications of the Latter-day Saints has especially equipped him to respond to claims that have not been dealt with in other Christian books on the subject.